ESMERELDA'S TRAVEL TALES
Humourous Adventures of Esmerelda Perkins
Book Three

Sheila Carnegie

ISBN-13: 978-1548921699
ISBN-10: 1548921696

DEDICATION

For all vicarious travellers
who seek the lighter side of life

ACKNOWLEDGMENTS

with sincere gratitude

Editor: Jan Myers

Copy Editor: Stephen Fine

Designer: Jan Myers

Cover: Alton Johnson

Publishing and Marketing: LJM Publishing, LLC

Cotacachi Writers Group for support and encouragement

Anonymous readers

FOREWORD

Authors Note: Although these stories are based on actual travel experiences, they remain fictional; please forgive Esmerelda if she has taken liberties in her physical descriptions or character portrayal; any resemblance to persons living or dead is purely coincidental.

Contents

IT'S ALL IN A WORD

"Don't gobblefunk around with words."
Ronald Dahl, The Big Friendly Giant

I'm at the Manzanillo airport, surrounded by swaying palms and scented scarlet hibiscus, absorbing solar warmth, rotating one hip to a mariachi beat, inching forward in the taxi line. Finally, it's my turn. Then I see him. There before me, unfolding himself from the vehicle, is one of the most gorgeous male creatures ever to cross my path. He is what women much younger than I would call a 'real hunk'. Hell, actually he is what I'd call a real hunk.

By this time, having landed ten minutes previous, I've observed that Mexican men come in at least two basic body types. The first type is doe-eyed, round, pot-bellied, with shoe-polished chocolate chipmunk cheeks, and chalk-white enameled grins... perfect for toothpaste commercials. The other is the tall, slender type before me now... elegant, mysterious, caramel-faced hombres, with chiseled Roman features, flashing ebony eyes, and coal-black silver-smattered curls.

"Wow!" The air is sucked out of me. My chin drops; my vocal cords struggle; words fail to emerge.

I always was a sucker for the dark-haired, swarthy type. Of course, there was that blonde with the Kookie Ed Burns ducktail an eon or so ago... and then that freckled, hazel-eyed, sandy-haired guy... sort of a half-assed redhead. Now he was a **huge** mistake. And then, more recently, the bald-headed fellow with eyes as blue as cornflowers. Come to think of it, I've **never** had a tall, dark, handsome guy in my life... I mean not in **that** way.

"Wow!" "Wow!!!" I have lost concentration. I am battling hyperventilation.

"Hussy!" erupts a voice from some cavern in my brain. "Shameless old lady!"

I snap back, "I might be old but I'm not yet cold! Besides, who says sixty-year old women are without passion or desire? Even if absent-minded, or prune-wrinkled or pear-shaped?"

I am shaken from my stupor by a sexy Belafonte-like rumble rolling from deep within the throat of this Adonis before me. He is speaking to me! In Spanish. Instinctively, I know it's something romantic.

Something like, "Can I help you?" or "Would you like a taxi?"

My Spanish at this point is minimal. Hell, to be honest, it is pretty much non-existent. Except, of course, for a few words essential to one's survival, words like *'cerveza, por favor'*, which I readily learned in Cuba years ago. Beer, please. And *'vino tinto'*. Red wine. Both necessities of life as far as I'm concerned.

Flustered, I probe the recesses of my brain to find the precise words I have rehearsed for this very moment. *"Quiero llevarte a mi casa, por favor"*.

Adonis raises his eyebrows, wrinkles his brow, struggles to suppress twitching at the corners of his mouth, spasms that threaten to metamorphose into a full-fledged grin. The woman behind me guffaws, gives me a 'thumbs up'.

Puzzled, I try again. *"Quiero que me lleva a mi casa, por favor"*.

This time I apparently get it right. Then it dawns on me as I mentally replay the two statements. Not so different. A word or two out of place. Huge difference in meaning though. Huge, huge distinction between "I'd like you to take me to my house, please," and "I'd like to take you home, please."

I mumble the guesthouse address. Gracefully, he nods, hoists my luggage, opens the rear door. We ride in silence... except for my repeated muttering. To myself. "Esmerelda Perkins, you *"idiota"*. And rehearsing, under my breath, *"No hablo español. No hablo español."* I do not speak Spanish. This is in preparation for what I am certain lies ahead. Adonis, eyes narrowed, closely scrutinizes me in the rearview mirror. So begins my Mexican vacation.

****

That was the first but, unfortunately, far from the last of what might be termed language-related incidents. Language-related incidents that may well have become international incidents. None of which were my fault. I mean not really. Without question, the language was to blame. Spanish, after all, does have similar sounding words with different meanings. In fact, Spanish vocabulary differs among countries and among regions within one country. So in no way was I culpable.

How was I to know, for example, when I planted myself at a shoe shop entrance, when I deliberately sniffed the air, inhaling the delicious scent of fresh leather and saddle soap... how was I to know, when I gestured my arm towards rows and rows of incredibly soft, impeccably hand-crafted shoes... how was I to remember that 'many shoes' translates as *'muchas botas'* rather than *'muchas bostas'*... 'much dung'?

Furthermore, was it my fault when, intending to compliment a bejeweled, corseted and elegantly garmented, silver-haired Spanish lady on her exquisitely hand-embroidered shawl... her *'chala'*... I instead murmured *"chalada"*, 'crazy'? Was it my fault that I didn't remember the word for pine nuts *(piñones)* and instead asked the waiter if he had any *'piojos'*, (lice)? Or that I forgot the distinction between *'colorante'* (colouring) and *'colgante'* (hanging out)? Although I really should have clued in to that one when the vendor kept checking his zipper.

And I definitely wasn't responsible for getting booted out of the clothing shop. That was really unfair. In fact, I'm still not entirely certain what happened there.

I am browsing. *"Solamente mirando,"* I tell the rotund shopkeeper who resembles a hairy-chested garden gnome with oily, slicked back hair and an unbuttoned, tropical shirt sporting fuschia hibiscus and jade-coloured palm fronds. Just looking. *"Solamente mirando. Mucho que mirar."* Lots to look at.

Mexican clothing shops differ from those in North America. Vivid colours. Brilliant lime greens. Flaming hot pinks. Fluorescent tangerines. Deep sea turquoises. Yellow so sunny it hurts your eyes. Primarily one-of-a-kind items, not necessarily arranged by size or style. Frills and flounces. Elaborate hand-embroidery. No two patterns alike and no consistent sizes. *'Mucho que mirar.'* Much to look at.

I wander among the racks, checking one garment or another, for style, size, price. He follows, asks me something. I have absolutely no idea what. *"Solamente mirando"*, I reply. Just looking. He tries again and again. *"Solamente mirando"*, I repeatedly mutter. He shrugs, scowls, shadows me.

I am annoyed... I detest being watched when I shop, scrutinized as though I were a shoplifter, a *ladrona*, a thief. I move behind him. He turns. Again I position myself behind him. Having abandoned all communication attempts, we continue circling each other, as cattle-buyers at an auction or vultures stalking prey.

Then I spot the dress. I covet this piece of finery... an elegant, versatile, classic black silk number... one that might be accessorized to suit any occasion from a poolside party to a formal dinner. The correct size, sexy to boot. Perfect. I've hit the jackpot.

I approach him. Purposefully. Confident. *"Quiero comprar tu mejor bestida"*, I beam. I want to purchase your finest dress. *"Estoy lista."* I am ready.

At least, that is what I'm certain I said.

He blanches, sputters. Tight-lipped, he spews curses. I know they are curses because I know *perra* is the word for bitch, and I've already learned that *chalada* means crazy. He grabs my elbow, steers me towards the door. I resist. He drags me, pushes me. Clutching the dress, I dig in my heels, skid along the floor like a recently-launched water skier. It has taken me several hours to find this treasure. I'm not leaving without it.

"No hablo español," I stammer, shrugging, squeezing out a few tears, *"no hablo español."*

His tirade continues, *"Perra chalada! Ladrona! Puta!"*

A rather intense crowd gathers, pointing, babbling, clucking, questioning. Numbers grow. The volume increases. I speculate. Are criminals stoned in Mexico? Are they tarred and feathered or just thrown into scorpion-fraught dungeons? I mean what do they do with bitches deigned to be crazy? Let alone thieves and harlots?

Suddenly, a solid, stately, middle-aged woman, in a black linen business-like suit with a crisp white blouse, dark hair tidily knotted at her neck, emerges from the crowd. She has a commanding presence, is obviously an organized, orderly, and a take-charge type of person. I instantly sense the dress and I will emerge safely from this conundrum. My perception is accurate. She introduces herself as Carlotta Munoz, extends her hand and offers to translate, to mediate.

As she speaks in turn to each of us, the crowd hangs on every word, their faces swinging in unison first The last few hours before we reach Hanoi are quiet. We both have our own silent thoughts as we prepare to go separate ways. In our week together, we have grown to be towards me, then him, then me. Back and forth, like a pendulum on a Grandfather clock or a metronome.

After several minutes, to the relief of everyone, including the now chattering, chuckling, gradually dispersing crowd, the problem is clarified. He claims I did not say, *"Quiero compra el mejor bestida. Estoy lista."* I want to buy your finest dress. I am ready. He insists I said, *"Quiero comprar, lo mejor bestia. Estoy lista."* I want to buy you, you fine beast. I am ready.

Now, be honest. Would you notice the difference in pronunciation between *mejor bestida* and *mejor bestia?* And how was I to know that *bestida* is really *vestida...* it sounds like a *'b'* to me when pronounced by the locals. Do you not think he could have given me the benefit of the doubt? Come on. I mean really. He isn't even tall, dark, and handsome. Maybe the guy is hard of hearing. Hell, give me a break! Ah well, I have learned a new word *puta.* Harlot.

Subsequently, I avoid Mexican shops. Especially clothing shops. I say nothing. I purchase only items I can point to, touch, count, pick up. And from beach vendors, I choose some stunning red coral beads to complement my exquisite, sexy black dress.

****

The clincher, however, was the fiasco with the street vendor selling *dulces de coco.* *Dulces de coco.* Coconut candy. No way was I accountable for that injustice. Absolutely not.

"Dulces de coco?" he asks.

"Si, por favor," I reply.

"Muchos o poco?"

"Un poco." A little.

"Cuantos cuesta?" How much does it cost?

He names a price. I whistle. Sounds like a lot for a little coconut candy. Especially in Mexico. Must be a rare treat. Or maybe he misunderstood.

"Mota?" he asks.

Now I know that *mota* means a small piece. Why is he asking again? *"Si, mota. Mota is bueno,"* I answer. A small piece is good... especially at his quoted price. At this point I am very proud of my ability to communicate so well. I count out my pesos and place them in his extended palm. He nods.

From behind me, a hand reaches out and clamps my shoulder. I turn... and realize that the vendor has not nodded to me, he has nodded to someone behind me. Two grim-faced, charcoal-uniformed, crested and capped *policia,* both short, round, one pock-marked, the other lined and tired. Holstered guns slung across their hips, handcuffs dangling from leather belts. I fail to understand their words. Nothing that is except *mota... mota* and *coco.* Their intention is clear. They motion me to go with them. Both mean business.

Now how the hell was I to know that *mota* also means 'weed'? Or that *dulces de coco* was a euphemism used by local coke dealers?

Once settled in the station, I contemplate trying to explain this to them, the *policia*, but settle for an alternate strategy.

"No hablo español," I reiterate. In response to every question, whether or not I understand a word, *"No hablo español,"* again and again, like a parrot practicing for its first recital. (I don't know the words for 'I need a lawyer').

They demand my passport, which happens to be buried beneath the silky lingerie in my room. Be damned if I'm going to try to explain that one and risk once more being labeled a harlot.

"No hablo español," I shake my head and hand over my driver's license.

They pass it back and forth, peering, examining, scrutinizing more closely than one might a suspected counterfeit bill.

"Colom-beeah?" one questions.

"Si. British Columbia, Canada," I answer.

"Breeteesh Colom-beeah? Donde?"

"Old Toad Island", I say.

He arches his eyebrows, gestures towards me, nods at his partner, *"Esa figura. Un otra una."* That figures. Another one.

This afternoon, I skip beachcombing. Not by choice. Time suspends itself as we wait for a translator to arrive from a neighbouring city. My episodic attempts to meditate are fragmented by recurring visions of filthy, scorching, scorpion-laden Mexican jails. Starvation. Leg irons. Whippings. Torture. Guillotines. Are other Old Toads there? Is that what happened to the couple who failed to return to the island last year? I mean what happens to accused drug buyers? Or dealers? Will I recognize cellmates? Suddenly I aspire to become a thief, or even a harlot.

Around the time I should have been communing with yet another spectacular sunset, sipping a pre-dinner margarita from my balcony hammock and ruminating about the burdens of doing nothing, the translator strides through the door. There before me stands an organized, business-attired, competent, take-charge woman. I stare. My chin drops. She is, in fact, the same woman who rescued me from the irate shopkeeper. The one and the same Carlotta Munoz. An angel in disguise. This truly is a 'happy hour' of a different nature.

I stifle cheers. For fear this might be misinterpreted, I restrain myself from uninhibitedly

dancing, uncontrollably leaping about the room, unabashedly throwing myself into her embrace, or the arms of the *policia*. However, once again, I sense I will escape this situation intact.

Once again I do. Oh yes, there are grins and stifled guffaws and sideways glances as she relays the tale of the accused *ladrona* and *perra* and *puta*. These words I understand. In the end, however, the policia apologize, shake my hand with the dignity and respect extended to little old Mexican ladies and, now apparently, towards little old Breeteesh Colom-beeah ladies who *habla no español*. No *español* and no *mota*.

Later, from my balcony, as the golden orb slid into scarlet dusk, I poured a double rum, toasted both the translator and my good fortune. I swear, for the first time in more years than I remember, I swear that had I possessed a mota de mota, it may well have gone up in smoke.

****

I'm back at the Manzanillo bus station, hailing a taxi to the airport. There before me, once more unfolding himself from his taxi, is one of the most gorgeous male creatures to ever cross my path. You got it... 'my Adonis', the one and the same. Avoiding direct eye contact, we both nod and smile in recognition. As we near the journey's end, after some cautious small talk, and mutual voracious grinning, I ask him in perfect Spanish, "Now would you like to come home with me?"

He chuckles, eyes dancing, then responds, "Yes, I would very much like to come home with you; however, my wife might object." In perfect English. Our amusement is mutual.

"Shameless old lady," admonishes my alter ego, *"Puta! Harlot!"* I ignore her. I conclude in fact that she is likely to blame for the still elusive tall, dark, handsome guy of my dreams.

Furthermore, as my mother always told me, "What are dreams if you haven't any?" *Soñar.* To dream. Not so different from *soltar.* To set free.

Tener sueño. To have a dream. Not so different from *tomar suerte.* To take a chance. I refuse to abandon dreams… and chances are for the taking. I do, however, vow to improve my Spanish.

A STRANGER IN TOWN

"There are no strangers here, only friends you haven't yet met".

William Butler Yeats

The taxi skids sideways across the ice to a sudden stop in front of a paint-peeled, dilapidated building. My neck stiffens with apprehension... the sort of instinct that tells one to turn and run. *Get the hell out of here, Esmerelda.* Before it's too late.

"This is the Churchill Hotel?"

"Hhmmph," snorts the driver, wiping his runny nose across his sleeve. "The one and only," he mutters, hand-rolled cigarette dangling from his nicotine-stained lip, bobbing up and down as he speaks. "Only a stranger in town would ask. The other one burned down." He gestures his snotty sleeve toward a vacant lot or, rather, a lot empty but for piles of snow-covered rubbish, dregs of what must have been a previous building. Charred board fragments and blackened two-by-fours poke skyward through the white blanket, as though threatening to betray some shame disguised beneath.

A stranger in town. Yes, for certain. At this moment that is precisely how I feel, a foreigner in a foreign land. Although I haven't departed my own country, this landscape is completely unfamiliar to me.

"Yes, I know. That is why I've booked in here. Thank you." I hand him the fare with a substantial tip. He stuffs it into his pocket, says nothing, opens the trunk, plops my luggage on the frozen tundra. "Welcome to Churchill, Manitoba," I murmur under my breath. It is April, a lifetime ago.

17

I struggle forward, snow crunching beneath my boots, set down my suitcase, push open the creaking door. It takes my eyes a moment to adjust to the dim light within.

The obviously once-grand but now-shabby lobby has huge varnished beams and a dark, oiled wooden floor, the kind that reminds me of my schoolroom when I was a kid. In the autumn when we returned from summer vacation it was always to the reek of fresh oil. Now I almost expect to hear crickets chirping, a sound I associate with that smell. Instead, I am greeted by the ruckus from an adjoining restaurant, the kind of commotion typical of a party well underway.

With a deep breath, mustering courage, I saunter to the reception desk and wait. No one comes. I ring the desk bell... a pinging sound that also reminds me of that prairie schoolroom long ago, of the teacher calling the class to attention. I wait. No one attends. I ring again, wait, ring a third time.

Now you must understand that at this point in my life I am not the Esmerelda into whom I have since metamorphosed. At this point in my life, I am young, naïve, untravelled, somewhere between the larvae and pupae stages of life, so to speak. I lack the nerve I have since gained. I lack the bravado to shriek at the top of my lungs, which I have since been known to do, "Where the hell is everybody? Out on the bloody trapline?" I lack the gumption to demand, which I have since been known to do, "Is this a service or a charity?" In retrospect, that was probably a good thing.

I ring yet again. Finally, a seemingly disinterested, olive-skinned, black-haired woman, garbed in a floral print dress stretched tightly across her more-than-ample bosom, waddles to the desk. "Yah?"

I state my name, that I have a reservation.

"No, no such reservation," she barely glances at the roster.

"Yes, I have a reservation. I am with the Careers Program and I made the reservation myself."

"No, no reservation."

What I lack in experience and dynamism, I make up for in persistence. "I know I have a reservation. I called at least three weeks ago and made it myself. Please check again."

She scrutinizes the roster. "No, sorry, no reservation. No room."

Panic rises in my throat. No other hotels, no one to call, in fact, no one I really know in Churchill. And it is damn cold outside at night, even in April. "Well, then, someone must have made a mistake. Will you please get the manager?"

She hesitates, furrows her brow, shrugs, shuffles from the room, and in a few minutes returns with a disheveled, grey-faced, wrinkled man in bedroom slippers, his grubby long johns visible at his ankles. A rumpled red plaid flannel shirt reveals a hairy chest and huge white belly. His hair is tousled as though he has been awakened from sleep. He is so ashen I am worried he might not live through our conversation.

His bloodshot eyes squint at the roster. "No, sorry, no reservation."

For each of his claims that there is no reservation, I insist that one had been made, until he finally folds. "Never mind. We'll find a room. Leave your luggage here. You wait there," he points in the direction of the commotion, "in the coffee shop. I'll call you when a room is ready."

With some anxiety and skepticism bordering total mistrust, I abandon my luggage. It is mid-afternoon by now, well past checkout time, and I wonder how a room can be manufactured if none is available. However, I concede, "In the meantime, is there a washroom I might use?"

He gestures to a far, dark corner of the lobby. I approach the 'Ladies'. The door, which hangs partially off its hinges, cannot be closed. I turn; however, both the man and woman have vanished from the lobby.

Reluctant to be on display to anyone entering the hotel, or its lobby, I move to the 'Men's', knock, and wait. No response. Knock again. Still no response. I slide forward, unobserved, lock the door, and straddling the toilet seat, quickly become more comfortable. I never really believed anyone caught anything from toilet seats. However, if even a remote possibility exists, I instinctively know this would be the place.

Now I will wait. Entering the coffee shop is an event in itself. One must first part clouds of acrid cigarette smoke, as thick as rolling night fog on Haworth's cobblestone streets in the English moors. Choking, eyes stinging, wishing I had a gas mask, I slide into the first empty chair I see, peer around the room. I question whether I have walked in on a support group for chain-smokers. No wonder the other hotel burned to the ground. I hope this isn't the night for a similar event at this one.

The coffee is so strong, black and bitter, it might well have been reheated from a few days previous. Two or three sips later, a very short, skinny, unkempt, leathered-faced Inuit, in scruffy jeans, parka and filthy, fur-topped, beaded mukluks, gingerly weaves his way across the room. He stops at my table. He leans over me, staggers and clutches the table to steady himself. The heavy stench of whisky is unmistakable, overpowering. He affectionately throws an arm around my shoulders and with his black, slitted and bloodshot eyes leveled a couple of inches from my face, he peers directly into my own.

"Well, shello honeysh," he slurs, "I ain't sheen you in a lonnnnggg time! Where... where wersh you?" This is followed by an onslaught of babble I fail to understand, possibly Inuit.

I don't know how to answer. I don't know how to tell him where I have been. Or why I should. I want to tell him how much I wish I were not here at this moment.

I try, in vain, to explain I am not who he thinks. He pays no attention. For each of my claims that I have never met him before, he insists I am one of his 'honeysh'. Is this a nightmare... something unreal... something I am viewing through Alice's Looking Glass?

He blocks my getaway. It likely doesn't cross his mind that one of his 'honeyshesh' might want to escape. My desperation must be apparent. A second clean-cut heavier-set Inuit, deliberate in his movements, sets down his coffee, stands, winks at me, crosses the room, and with a few words I don't understand, guides the first fellow back to his table. After a few more sips, I abandon my coffee, propel my way back through the smoke to the lobby. It is still empty.

My suitcase, however, is still here. A blessing. Perhaps even a miracle. I wait. And wait. I consider calling my work contact, but see no pay phones and have no clue where her office is located. It isn't as though there are street names and numbers. Besides, she is a stranger. I have no idea how she would react or if she is presently in her office. It is now late afternoon. I know the plane has long since left. I know there are no other flights until tomorrow. I again ring the desk bell.

It seems that I have waited for hours... perhaps because I have. Thoughts ramble. Did I leave my itinerary at work? How long can I stay awake? Will my family search for me? Might I sleep on the floor behind the front desk? Perhaps I should make some notes, leave pictorials like Hudson's men did on the nearby rocks. Before they disappeared. Am I becoming incoherent?

Eventually the 'manager' drags himself into the room, "Ah, yah, I was just going to call you ; we have a room for you." I shoot straight up, suddenly alert. He passes me a key clearly imprinted 'Room # 5'. I hope he knows from the relief in my voice just how grateful I am. I glance downward, actually consider kissing his soiled, slippered feet. For a moment, that is, for only a very, very brief moment.

I stagger upstairs, one step at a time, dragging my suitcase that grows heavier by the second. I briefly entertain the thought that a corpse has been stashed. Maybe that's whose room I am getting. In the dim hallway light, I fumble with the key. This door, too, creaks open. It seems to me that some of the oil on the lobby floor might have been used on door hinges.

I feel for the light switch, flick it on, gasp, back out of the room, all in one motion. There is a man in the bed! A nude man! Well, except for the sheet covering his bottom, a nude man! He stirs not a hair, but is snoring, rumbling like an approaching freight train. Well thank god, at least he is alive. And his rhythm is amazing… I mean one could write poetry or conduct music to such rhythm!

It isn't until years later I realize this was one of those moments that could have, in an instant, changed my life forever. I mean what if he had awakened? What if I had awakened him? Introduced myself? Asked why he was sleeping in 'my' bed and how did he get there? What was he doing in Churchill? Perhaps he was a biologist? A travel photographer? Polar bears commonly wandered into town this time of year. Or a Greek shipping magnate? After all Churchill is a port. To think I could have ended up spending my life sailing the Mediterranean in a diamond-studded bikini. But if that were the case, what was he doing in such a sleazy hotel? Of course, he could have asked the same about me. And god forbid, I cannot even imagine the consequences had I complimented him on his incredible rhythm! Snoring, I mean.

Back in the lobby, once more I summon the manager, politely protest sharing the room with an unknown male. Sure, I possess inherent inner gumption that is biding its time and that is certain to emerge at some point in the future. But tonight I am defeated, despondent. Besides, I can hardly afford getting tossed out onto the frozen tundra in the throes of night. I am not that anxious to view polar bears, especially close up in darkness. Again, I wait. I am exhausted. I fight sleep that threatens to envelop.

In the coffee shop, I order a second cup of black, tarlike eye-opener. This time, since my newly-found Inuit 'boyfriend' has slumped into oblivion in one corner of the room, leaning like a wet mop against one wall, I need no intervention on my behalf. Thus, I peacefully demolish a mooseburger (complete with mayo, mustard, tomato, fried onions, cheese and pickles), pick away at a few greasy french-fries which I slather with ketchup, hoping to disguise their palatability, or rather lack thereof. Again I wait. And wait.

I have given up trying to determine what I am supposed to learn from this. A test of patience has long since passed. Like a prisoner in solitary confinement, or one kidnapped by a cult, maintaining brain function has become my immediate goal. Finally, sometime during what seems to have been a very long nightmare, I am summoned to a second room. I feel numb. On automatic pilot, once more I trek up the stairs, once more haul my suitcase, a burden that seems to have attached itself in the manner of a parasite.

Fighting mental fog that threatens to eradicate cognition and conscious thought, I puzzle over the availability of a vacant room at this hour. Might it too be occupied? I check every corner. I check the closet. Peer under the bed. However, this time the room is devoid of humans, though I cannot be certain it lacks all living creatures. The crumpled sheets indicate the bed has not been touched since its last occupant. There is no way of knowing how long ago that might have been. It is entirely possible that someone is locked in the hallway bathroom. Or perhaps someone has been evicted to the freezing night. Worst of all, it is entirely possible some guy currently slugging a beer in the downstairs bar will later be joining me, in the same manner that I was encouraged to join another occupant, just a few hours ago.

Desperate for sleep, I yank the bedspread over the sheets, lock the door, jam a chair under the knob. I'm taking no chances. Fully clothed, I lay atop the bed. Covered with my parka. In time, I dose off, with visions flitting through my mind, nightmares about people getting bedbugs or lice or scabies from unclean sheets, tales about people murdered in their sleep. I sleep fitfully. Why on earth could I not have conjured dreams about the Greek shipping magnate?

The next day, during a business meeting, the reason for my Churchill visit, I am asked where I stayed. Perhaps the dark circles under my eyes or crumpled clothes clue in other meeting participants. Or even worse, perhaps I carry the odor of oiled floors and stale, unwashed bedsheets. My response prompts an exchange of knowing glances among meeting participants. It is then explained that, since the other hotel burned, it is common practice for community visitors to rent beds in the Alcohol Treatment Center.

Faster than Donovan Bailey racing the 100-meter, swifter than Ben Johnson on steroids, I whip back to the hotel, gather my luggage and check out. One of the women I met earlier waits in her car, motor running, exhaust vaporizing in the cold. My feet dance across packed snow; my suitcase weighs nothing at all.

That night I sleep like a talcum-bottomed newborn on comfortable, clean sheets. That night I dream of daisy-filled meadows, serene pine-scented woodlands, huge bowls of ginger ice cream adorned with dark chocolate chunks. And a Greek shipping magnate. Certainly, that night I am likely the most blissful, contented person to ever sleep in a detoxification unit. Furthermore, I am no longer a stranger in town.

Sheila Carnegie

A MEASURE OF FAITH

"Doubt is a pain too lonely to know that faith is his twin brother."

Kahlil Gibran

I'm on a bus somewhere between Manzanillo and Armeria, enroute to Cuyutlan. I soon realize that before embarking I should have considered alternatives. Like a taxi. Or hitchhiking. But I had been assured of the reliability of the Mexican transit system. "Efficient," they said. "Economical." "Comfortable," they encouraged. "Sit back, Esmerelda, sit back and relax, watch TV," they advised. "Safe," they reassured. However, on this, what is otherwise a tranquil, sunny Sunday morning with cotton fluff floating across clear blue sky, I clutch the edge of the seat, gnaw my lip, and wish I had tucked a fifth of tequila in my backpack. Hell, this is a journey that promises to invoke fear in the most courageous of self-sacrificial terrorists on a suicide mission.

The stocky, caramel-skinned, uniformed driver, humming to the tune of *Amazing Grace*, whips the bus around mountainside hairpin curves like a madman racing the Indy 500, sometimes passing on solid lines. Frozen into silence, I fixate upon rosary beads dangling from the windshield, swinging wildly, whacking the crucifix on one side and the Virgin Mary on the other. I realize this guy actually believes symbolism will protect us from his erratic and maniacal driving. I become even more terrified. He, however, is fearless.

I've already learned that faith is a big deal in Mexico. After all, most of its citizens, if not all, are practicing Catholics. No shortage of faith here. For example, in La Manzanilla, the crocodile lagoon is located

27

in the middle of the village. On one side a fence separates their territory from the street. The other three sides are demarcated by yellow ticker tape... the kind police use to block off a crime scene. No one seems concerned about this. No one seems to have considered that ticker tape is not exactly a secure barrier. A matter of faith, I conclude.

I have no idea if or how the crocs know they are supposed to remain within that area. I am told they stray only at night, cross the deserted beach to swim in the ocean. I am not eager to authenticate this rumour. To be honest, when in the vicinity, even at high noon, I give their territory a wide berth and keep my eyes peeled, just in case some of them are slow learners. Or in the event they fail to understand the disillusionment that might result from misplaced faith of fellow Mexicans.

How could I have possibly known that today, on this trip to Cuyutlan, a tiny, peaceful, virtually undiscovered village on a West-coast, black sand beach, my faith will once again be tested? However, here I am, staring death in the eye.

Numerous crosses, thrusting erratically from the dirt, adorned with dust-coated, multi-hued plastic flowers, denote death by the roadside. Others can be seen where the roadside drops vertically into steep-sided ravines. I count crosses. In some places there are too many to count... they blur as we speed past. I realize, however, that the number of crosses is frequently greater than the number of people that would fit into one vehicle. Even a truck, unless it were a semi-trailer, that is. The more I think about this, the more certain I am that only bus disasters could precipitate so many crosses in one spot.

This insight is less than comforting. Grim-faced and white-knuckled, I brace myself, hang on as we sway to and fro with the weaving vehicle. I visualize the bus careening over the edge, rolling to the bottom of the gulch... in slow motion, one turn at a time, rousing clouds of choking dust, occasionally dispelling ragdoll-like figures from newly created cavities in the gradually disintegrating vehicle.

My stomach knots. I imagine the cross that will mark my grave. I picture a spray of flowers. Birds of Paradise. I want Birds of Paradise. I'll settle for no less. No one dare gift me with plastic... I want the real thing or nothing. Or perhaps my cross could bear tribute to some of my accomplishments. Or include an inscription naming my favourite charities.

Suddenly it dawns on me that I have no friends or relatives in Mexico. Who will erect a cross let alone bring flowers or engrave inscriptions? No one. I shiver. There must be innumerable other tourists who have met their roadside Waterloo without tribute. There must be incalculable, inestimable fatalities that go unacknowledged. Deaths without grave markers. Maybe double or even triple those tangible. This realization drastically lowers the probability of one safely reaching one's destination, of my ever setting foot on the Cuyutlan beach.

A tremor shudders through me and plunges like an icy stone, settles in my gut. Is this what is meant by cold terror? I am now aware that several previously lounging, drowsing passengers have bolted upright like stick soldiers on duty. They murmur. Finger rosary beads. A skinny, wrinkled, leather-skinned, white-haired man mutters on his cell phone, tells someone where his last will and testament is kept. To whom he bequeaths his gold cross and chain. I am not alone in my fear.

Now, I should make something clear... I am not a Catholic. Hell, I am not even a religious person. But I figure what exactly have I got to lose? I follow the lead of other passengers. I clasp the beads I purchased beachside yesterday, the tiny vividly multi - hued stone - like shells adorning my neck. Surely they'll do in an emergency. I cross myself, murmur Hail Mary's and finger my makeshift rosary in unison with everyone else.

I am fortunate. Weak-kneed, trembling, I disembark at Armeria. The others proceed onward to Colima, which, I later discover, is a far more snaking, treacherous route. The bus driver, his Colgate smile intact, resumes his seat at the wheel, totally oblivious to the terror he instills. He begins to hum. *Oh Lamb of God I Come.* His faith is unflappable. I suppose, since I have arrived safely, I should concede that perhaps he is on to something. As the bus spins from the curb, spits up gravel, passengers peer backwards, craning their necks, waving, beseeching. Several of them, shrugging and sighing, settle back, resign themselves to fate, once again clutch rosary beads to their breasts, once more rely upon faith for salvation.

Faith... relinquishing the illusion of control and overcoming the power of fear, following each breath to the depths of one's soul, flowing with intuition and passion and inner assurance. The rooster that crows in the dark believing dawn will follow. Homeless street dogs on daily rounds, trusting they will find scraps and morsels sufficient to sustain life for one more day. Blossoms that unfold in early spring, knowing summer's warmth is sure to follow. The newborn who never questions the presence of his mother's breast. Faith, stepping blindly into tomorrow, moving forward in the direction of the pueblo, knowing that home lies somewhere over the horizon.

On the street, someone points me toward the station where awaits the Cuyutlan-bound bus. I shake my head back and forth like a dog does when he has nabbed but wants to rid himself of a snake. Instead, I hail a taxi, and travel the last few kilometers, grateful for life... for life and for rosary beads. It seems I have yet to work a little more on faith.

ESMERELDA GOES TO ESMERALDAS

"Your living is determined not so much by what life brings you as by the attitude you bring to life; not so much by what happens to you as by the way your mind looks at what happens."

Kahlil Gibran

Drenched to the bone, we are slumped at a paint-peeled, picnic-style slab wooden table, plopped on a bench that has settled into inches of sand beneath our bare feet. The pouring rain drips through overhead thatch, gusts of wind whip through the open-walled restaurant, which we've been told is *The Bamboo Inn*. There is no sign to indicate its name. We are not supposed to be here. It isn't even the right place. Our Capri pants and protruding legs, which seem as though they belong to someone else, are splattered in muck. We have long since removed our sandals, mud-heavy and useless in this monsoon. Our elbows rest on the table, our heads cradled in our hands. How the hell did we get here? And how the hell do we get out of this mess?

Part One: In the Beginning

My friend Sheila from Tree Frog Island insists it was my brainwave... this trip to Esmeraldas in northwest Ecuador, near the Colombian border. I maintain it was hers. Funny, how memories differ, how each of us is certain she is correct. She says I wanted to find out if I was named after Esmeraldas or it was named after me... after all, which of us is older is questionable. But that's silly. Esmerelda is not even spelled the same as Esmeraldas. I maintain that she wanted to check out the possibility of finding emeralds, or adventure, or a guy. Perhaps all three. My memory is a little fuzzy… but I swear it was her idea.

Hell, it seemed like a good idea at the time. We both needed a break from the Canadian West Coast rainy season. We had separately visited Ecuador and had been entranced by something unexplainable, magical and mystical, imploring us to return. This time we planned to explore the Pacific Coast. Mind you, we had never travelled together before. That should have been a clue.

Oh yes, the trip started well enough. We met at the Vancouver Island airport. We decided to splurge this trip. Usually she or I travel by ferry to Vancouver and take the bus or sky train to the airport. Ferry crossings through the Strait of Georgia are spectacular… winding through islands… blues and greens… brisk breezes, sky and sea, occasional whale sightings, or some object one can pretend is a whale, a perfect beginning to a relaxing vacation. Except, of course, for ferry cuisine that is less than edible and costs twice the price of the fare (which is not exactly a bargain). I swear the West Coast clam chowder is made with ten-year-old tinned clams from Thailand, or clam-shaped pieces of rubber. No comparison whatsoever to freshly dug clams on Old Toad Island beach.

Both of us arrive early at the airport. We are alike in that way. Sheila reads or does Sudoku puzzles while we are waiting. I don't even pretend to know how those work. I people-watch, gather ideas for stories and characters. I've learned that you get the best information if you sit very still and pretend to see nothing, hear nothing, know nothing. No one ever clues in. They no doubt think I'm a harmless, little old lady trying to remember her whereabouts, just another senior rounding third base on her way to home, with lousy vision and hearing loss to boot. You think I haven't noticed? How, recently, people speak loudly, and slowly too, enunciating each word meticulously as though I am both deaf and mind-vacant. Comes with age, they think. The sad thing is they are probably right, but I'm not quite there yet. At least that's what I prefer to believe.

I glance around. Not too many characters here... we are so early. A young Asian guy, student I suspect, totally absorbed in his laptop and not particularly interesting, and an older guy, long-haired, graying and bearded. He could be from any one of the islands. He wears a partially shredded, khaki-coloured tee stretched across a bulging belly, jeans worn thin at the knees, a faded red plaid lumberjack shirt, and steel-toed boots. He is perched on a stool at the counter, nursing a beer and concentrating on tattoos that disappear beneath his rolled-up cuffs, that is, when he isn't eyeing the waitresses. Black leather is slung across his lap; a motorcycle helmet lies at his feet. He has potential, this guy... as a story character, that is. Don't get me wrong. He isn't my type... although I have long since forgotten who is.

I dig out my palm-sized notebook. No pen attached. I rummage through my backpack... I rarely carry a purse when travelling... still no pen.

"Have you a pen I can borrow?"

"Lord, Esmerelda, how can a writer forget her pen?" Sheila mutters, shakes her head, purses her lips, digs through her handbag and thrusts one toward me. Obviously, this isn't one of her more cheerful days.

I jot down details about this scruffy-looking biker. Little do I know that long before this trip is finished, he will fade in comparison to other characters we'll meet. And that Sheila's already less-than-generous attitude is bound to further deteriorate.

I turn my attention to the snack bar. Come to think of it, I am probably a 'foodie'. Food is my thing. Wine too, of course. You may have already guessed. Actually it's somewhat a miracle that I don't weigh three hundred pounds, though recently I seem to be heading in that direction. Now, the showcase before me is empty. Three women are discussing how to display their fare. One, mid-aged, spectacled, with strands of grey beginning to poke through her shortly-cropped, dark hair, in a slenderizing, navy pantsuit, appears to be in charge. The other two twenty-somethings, a bleached blonde and a streaked-purple brunette, are both wearing heavy makeup, tee shirts that appear to have shrunk at least two sizes, and butcher-style aprons over skinny tights that hug shapely little butts. Tacky, I think. Judging by the way the biker is ogling, I suspect he would disagree.

"Should we put the egg salad on the first shelf or the third?"

"First shelf."

"No, it would be better on the second. Ham and cheese should be on the first."

"What about the salmon?"

"Best on the second."

"Salmon should have its own place. Egg would be good with the ham and cheese. Complementary colours."

"Boring," I mutter silently. "Boring. Boring food. Why not something exotic? Enticing? Like Panini? Coquille? Escargot? Providing they really want sales? I mean who can't make a sandwich at home?"

Apparently reaching some agreement, one of the women removes saran-squished sandwiches from the fridge, passes them, one by one, to the second woman who hands them to the third. It reminds me of a line of volunteers desperately sand-bagging to barricade rising floodwaters.

The last woman gingerly fills shelves, meticulously arranges the sandwiches by type. The end result is that salmon gets the first shelf, beside the turkey salad, at least for a short time.

A second discussion ensues. Sandwiches are shuffled with the flurry of a casino blackjack dealer. Salmon moves to second with the tuna, BLT to first, egg salad to third... you get the picture. This reminds me of the Abbott and Costello skit, 'Who's on first?' Half an hour has now passed. Onward we move to the third discussion and re-arrangement. Salmon has returned to first, with turkey salad. What is wrong with these people? Suddenly I get it. They aren't selling a damn thing and have to justify their existence somehow. Unless, of course, they are practicing for Inuit bone games that keep one guessing as to what is where.

Finally, it seems settled. Oh, just a minute, not quite yet. The sandwiches are so well displayed there appears to be no room for the 'international section' that has been secreted in the refrigerator. I cannot believe this. They are pulling out spanikopita, samosas, sushi, wraps, stuffed pitas. Were they hoping we'd buy the sandwiches before we spied the other delicacies?

Another half hour of discussions and re-arrangements and they seem set to go. Just in time in fact... our flight is about to load.

"Want something to eat?" I query.

"Just ate a couple of hours ago," says Sheila. "Didn't you?"

"Yep. But it's a long way to Vancouver, Houston, Quito, then to Manta and on to Crucita. Once we get to South America you can be darn sure you won't find this selection. It seems the only sandwich Latin Americans know how to make is ham and cheese."

She nods. I demolish some sushi. We both tuck stuffed pitas in our carry-on luggage. It'll be more substantial than airplane snacks, usually a few salty 'bits' that one can eat in one 'bite', and a better alternative than mortgaging my house for a crummy airport meal.

The flight is nondescript, except for the spectacular view below, verdant fields, azure sparkling seas and snow-capped amethyst mountains, truly a bit of heaven. And the fact that the crew appear to be so damn young I cannot remember that far back. I wonder how many previous flights they could possibly have piloted. Hell, one doesn't start at age twelve. I console myself. At least I have managed a pretty decent last meal, just in case.

We set down on the tarmac in Vancouver. Smooth as Grand Marnier cheesecake. It's a brilliant sunny late afternoon. It is then I realize I don't have my prescription sunglasses. I have medications for every potential malady. I have band-aids, gauze, tourniquets, peroxide, eye refreshers, ear plugs, allergy creams, antibiotic creams, eye-drops, antacids, pain-killers, laxatives, diarrhea remedies, respirator, seasick prevention, anti-snake bite, flea repellant, adrenalin for bee stings. I have enough vitamins to feed the Canadian army. I have toothpicks, Q-tips, clothespins, safety pins, and bobby pins, though god knows why. Twine. I have trading pins, bubble soap, postcards, a compass in case I get lost, and an emergency alarm. But I have no damn sunglasses, prescription sunglasses that protect my post-cataract-surgery eyes now very sensitive to sunlight. No sunglasses. No sunglasses and no Spanish dictionary. Memories of Mexico wash over me, and the trouble I got into with the language. I sense another disaster in the making.

"Esmerelda," Sheila snarls, "I cannot believe this. Forgetting the things you need most. Where in the hell are we going to find prescription sunglasses?"

"We won't. The best we can do is to find some that clip onto my regular specs. And we won't likely find a dictionary either, so we will just have to go with the flow."

Sheila rubs her hand over her forehead, as though she wants to go home. Already. "Okay," she spits out the words, "let's first look for shades." This surprises me. I knew she was serious but believed her to be more patient, more patient and less uptight. I hope this isn't an omen of what lies ahead.

Lucky for us, or for me in particular, the Vancouver airport has lots of shades. Red. Tortoise-shelled. Hot pink. Tiger-striped tangerine. Oval, round, and square, huge and small. Fashionable. Dorky. Far out. I find a zebra-framed pair that looks great (in spite of what Sheila thinks). They will be fine, with exception of their ability to carve behind-ear grooves that are not likely to disappear in this lifetime. However, I dare not breathe a complaint or I may be travelling alone, an option that will grow more inviting in days ahead, although I am yet unaware.

The dictionary is another story. Once again, we will have to rely on my almost non-existent Spanish. My heart lurches with trepidation, for just an instant. Hell, after getting out of that mess in Mexico, I can deal with just about anything. Or so I think at the time.

Some thirty-four hours later, we arrive at Crucita, a seaside town on Ecuador's Pacific coast. The trip had its snags. Snags? Hell, it was god-awful. The downhill slide started in Vancouver, en route to Houston, when US Customs and Immigration officers, muttering something about the prohibition of meat across borders, confiscated our sandwiches. I didn't know egg salad and lettuce or falafel and bean sprouts could be classified as meat. It seems to me more likely they forgot to bring their lunch.

After that things rapidly deteriorated. I don't know what it is about Sheila... she triggers something in those 'guys'. She was searched four times before we even left Canada. Again in Houston, where they chipped her laptop keyboard, trying to pry it off. They removed the manicure set from her **checked** luggage. Was the nail file going to pop out of the suitcase mid-air and attack another suitcase? Or perhaps one of the officers needed a corkscrew?

In Quito, they hauled her out on the tarmac where they demanded she open her luggage in their presence, all the while eyeing her as though she were a terrorist. As though there was a bomb inside and she'd scream, "Oh no, no... don't open that! It'll explode!" Maybe it was the plastic jug of Canadian maple syrup that confused them. After all, they opened the seal and probed it with a chopstick-like piece of metal that did nothing but infuse bacteria. One gift down the pipe!

Before they allowed her through the final gate, they actually brought in a sniffer dog. Aptly labeled, he sniffed her carry-on bag, her computer, her purse and shoes. Even stuck his nose in her butt. You would think they could train those dogs to have better manners. I must admit the search worried me. I mean everyone knows that on Tree Frog Island (or Old Toad Island for that matter) there are more 'crops' than houses, growing in the least likely places, too... parks, Crown land, vacant properties. Who wouldn't have had some exposure to weed? Planted. Rolled. Smoked. That either of us got past that dog is a miracle in itself.

Needless to say, here we are, exhausted, in Crucita, described as a 'paradise on the spectacular white sand beach'. Well, true enough, one can see the beach if you crook your neck and peer through the window at an angle. And the beach probably would be white were it stripped of plastic and glass and paper garbage from the past weekend's fiesta.

Sheila is less than impressed. I am less than cantankerous, just grateful for a clean bed, bathroom, air conditioning and the fact that we have survived the first lap of what is rapidly becoming the trip to Hell. I'm conveniently ignoring the missed connection, lost luggage, pretzels that cost darn near a buck apiece, the airport bathroom in which we were locked for a good half hour, the taxi driver who took us to the wrong town, and the fact that our hotel has no hot water. Come to think of it, as Sheila keeps reminding me, even as I am falling asleep, we could have used that Spanish dictionary. Hell yes, I thought, had I brought it, I would throttle her with it this very minute.

As usual, after sleeping a dozen or so hours, the world appears brighter, to me, if not to Sheila. The hotel is a square-ish, four-tiered, white-painted concrete structure with a garden and pool in the back. Majestic palms, multi-coloured crotons, tumbling fuschia and tangerine bougainvillea provide both shade and ambience. We have a sense of the tropics and a measure of privacy. True enough, one can cross the pool with half a dozen strokes, but it is inviting, or it would be if the floating leaves and deceased critters were removed. No problem. With the ocean nearby, we are unlikely to use the pool anyway.

Part Two: The Die is Cast

Our breakfast, toasted ham and cheese sandwiches, accompanied by succulent lime-infused papaya chunks, juice and coffee, is served by the young, tall, slim, straight-postured, olive-skinned and casually dressed waiter, who checked us in the previous night. After we are served, I turn to Sheila. (We haven't spoken much this morning). "So do things appear better in the daylight?"

"Slightly," she grumbles. "Only… are you aware that the conditioner you loaned me (hers had been confiscated by Immigration) is a body lotion? Look at my hair!!!"

"Yeah, well, I wondered what happened to your hair. I suppose I forgot my conditioner too. I don't understand how that happened when I have at least half a dozen bottles of the stuff at home."

"Why so much conditioner?" she queries.

"Well when I'm shopping I usually remember that I need either shampoo or conditioner but forget which one. I inevitably buy the wrong one. Surely we can get some here," I shrug, hoping she will soon relax. Her persistently bad humour is beginning to annoy me.

She clucks her tongue. "How long do you…?" She cuts off her sentence midstream, focuses on a spot somewhere behind me.

I swivel. There stands a Latino man. Stocky. Round-bellied. Sneakered toes pointed out like a duck. Not tall, maybe 5'9". With the humidity, his silver-streaked coal black hair tumbles into ringlets. In spite of his physique, he is attractive, perhaps late 40's or early 50's, olive skinned with wide, doe-like brown eyes, long-lashed, and a huge Colgate smile. His tan shorts are mid-thigh in length; a brand-name black polo shirt is open at the neck. Gracious, charming, I sense, although he seems a little nervous, on edge.

"*Buenos dias. Como están*? How are you? I hope you sleep well. My name is Juan Tonio Garcia. I am hotel owner," he offers his hand, which I shake. Sheila withholds hers.

"Yes," I reply. "*Muy bien, gracias*. You speak English?"

"Sí," he replies, "but not very good. I be in Los Estados Unidos for much years when I am young. You understand okay?" He grins, glances at Sheila who seems frozen in her seat, mouth open, like a fish sucking air.

"*Muy bien*," I reply. "I understand very well. Your English is better than my Spanish. Are you Ecuadorian?"

"No. Colombian. From Medellin. But I live here for many years." He turns, beckons towards the doorway, from which a handful of figures emerge. "I like to present to you my staff. They all Colombian. You already meet Pedro. He is waiter. Sometimes he cook. He no speak English, but he treat you nice. I telephone another person in Colombia. She come tonight and she speak English. Be better for you." I am impressed... a personal attendant brought in just for us.

He waves an arm toward a man and woman, in matching psychedelic orange tee shirts, smiling side by side, like blooming geraniums. He is tall, bulky as a bar room bouncer, serious. She is tiny, voluptuous, with a spontaneous wide welcoming grin, as though she is honoured to be in our very presence. Both have gleaming black hair and ebony eyes. "May I present Jorge and *su esposa*... his wife, Maria. He is security and gardener. She clean, sometimes cook. You need something, you ask. They no speak English, but they smart and they good people. They get what you need or they call me."

Finally, he gestures towards a muscular, coal-eyed, twenty-ish hulk, with a single gold earring and spiked black hair, highlighted with a skunk-like blonde streak. His torn sleeveless muscle shirt reveals bulging biceps; cutoffs contain massive thighs and liberated bulky calves. Every inch of his skin, visible skin, that is, is tattooed with serpents, dragons, daggers, skulls and cross bones. A stylized phoenix rises above each. I try in vain to decipher all of them. Dangling from a heavy gold neck chain, strange as it seems, is a bird's feather, so delicate it threatens to float away. In time we learn this is his 'trademark' or 'symbol'.

"I present to you Diego. His name also Tattoos. He is bodyguard. He get me things and look after me. And you also," he grins again. "No be afraid. He harmless. Is possible you need something? Just ask. He know little bit English."

"*Mucho gusto*," I nod toward them. "Pleased to meet you. I am Esmerelda and this is my friend Sheila."

"Good to meet you," he responds. "Enjoy *desayuno*…your breakfast." He gestures toward the food. The others nod and smile. He swivels, waddles out. The others follow, chatting in Spanish, chirping like birds gathering for autumn migration.

The waiter, Pedro, soon returns with a coffee refill, stands nearby, straight, stiff, silent, watching and waiting, on 'call', much like a maitre d', in a posh dining establishment.

"Geez," Sheila mutters, shaking her head, "I can't believe this. Tony Soprano and his boys. How did you find this hotel?"

"Shhh," I warn, gesturing toward the waiter.

"He can't understand us," she lowers her voice. "Or at least so we are told."

"Oh, Sheila…just because they look like Mafioso doesn't mean they are. They seem like really nice people."

"Well, Esmerelda, so was Tony Soprano… when he wasn't slicing someone's throat."

"Relax. Make the best of this. We can rest here for a few days, keep our eyes open. Besides, these guys probably know how we can best get to Esmeraldas. It's pretty close to the Colombian border and they're Colombian."

"Well, we can't get there if we're held hostage. Of if we're not alive."

"Why on earth would they want to kill us? Or kidnap us? At our age, we are hardly candidates for prostitution." I gesture towards our sagging bodies. "You tell me who the hell would pay ransom?"

"For our cash? Our credit cards? Passports?"

I know her words are extreme, and that she is less of a risk-taker than I. But at this moment she is suspicious, bordering on paranoiac. However, she is also very intuitive and incredibly perceptive. She hangs out with psychics, and she once passed the test for the Canadian Security Intelligence Service (CSIS). I always thought she'd have made an amazing detective. After all, she nailed that cheating ex-spouse of hers. Set a trap and caught him cold, or hot, depending how one looks at it. When no one else could. So because I am reluctant to dismiss her concerns, she manages to spawn the ever-so-slightest seed of doubt in my mind.

We soon learn we are the only hotel guests. This seems strange, since there are eighteen rooms, and stranger still since most of the other hotels in town are booked solid. How are they keeping this place open, paying staff? Well, yeah, you may have already guessed what Sheila thinks. Money laundering. I suggest maybe the hotel is being discriminated against, based on stereotypes or the possibility that Ecuadorians object to Colombian business owners. But secretly I admit to myself that perhaps locals know something we don't.

The second day of our visit the Colombian, English-speaking (well sort-of-English-speaking) female 'manager', Carlotta, arrives. She is mid-thirties, polite, pleasant, soft-spoken, with long dark straight hair, tied back, and a characteristic mole on her cheek. As seems to be the custom with many Latin American women, she wears too much makeup and skintight, gaudy clothing that divulges more cleavage than dignity. Of course, it is possible that here bras are produced in only one size, as they seem to be in Mexico. Rows and rows of them hang in outdoor markets... hot pink, lime green, tangerine, grape... all the same size!

We have barely entered the restaurant when she descends upon us, like a preying buzzard, introduces herself, and proceeds to question us in a manner that after the first few minutes reminds one of the Gestapo. What are our names? Where do we live? How do we know each other? How did we come here? How long did it take? What do we work at? What am I writing? What do we want to see? What do we like to eat? Why did we choose this town? Why did we choose this hotel? (Though I must admit I, too, am beginning to ask that question and Sheila has never stopped asking it since that first night). Periodically, Carlotta leaves the room, goes into the office where the hotel owner is ensconced, returns, and shoots out in staccato-like fashion, the next series of questions. This pattern is repeated in following days.

During the next week or so, there are other strange occurrences. Diego-Tattoos, the 'body guard', asks if we would like accompaniment when we leave the hotel. On several mornings we spy Jorge, the 'security guard' tailing us along the beach, a block or so behind. In a half-assed discussion one day, about drug wars in Sicily and Pedro, the waiter, almost swallows his tongue when one day I mistakenly refer to 'Juan Tonio' as 'Don Juan Tonio'.
Carlotta and Pedro become very interested in my laptop images, especially those of my home, family (they frequently mention 'family'), and one of my sister-in-law garbed in black leather, perched on her Harley. "Policía," Pedro, who supposedly knows no English, gasps, "she policía?"

Carlotta holds her breath, carefully awaits my response. I pretend not to notice, carefully explain her recreational passion, outwardly overlook their obvious relief, or disbelief. Depending how well they act.

By the end of the first week we have become better acquainted with the manager and waiter, have established a sort of rapport, and are getting to know the owner. Some nights, Juan Tonio joins us at the bar, with whichever other staff happen to be present. He doesn't drink much, maybe a cold beer or two. He is quick-thinking, witty, fun to be around, has a broad base of knowledge, a unique view of local politics, and an interest in worldly affairs. He seems to welcome an opportunity to discuss issues in the Americas. Either that or he is corroborating his staff's assessment of us.

When I practice my Spanish on him, he chuckles gleefully, eyes twinkling, gently corrects me. "*Señora*, you say *tengo hambre* if you hungry. No *tengo hombre*. That says you have man." Or, "When you ask for *poco pecados*, *Señora*, you ask for little sins. Fish is *pescados*. Or, "Your ears are *orejas*. *Ovejas* are sheep." Or, "If you ask for pork, you say *el puerco*. If you ask for *la puerca*, you get the whole pig. How you say in English... the so... you know the mama... the so?" Other times he guffaws, says nothing. I enjoy the repartee between us and my Spanish is improving, or so I prefer to think. Sheila, on the other hand, nurses her drink, frowns, narrows her eyes, watches and listens, her silence hanging in the air like a judge's decision in a courtroom.

One evening Juan Tonio turns to me. "*Señora* Esmerelda," he hesitates, "you go to lagoon yet?"

"Lagoon? Where is that?"

"Lagoon maybe twenty minutes, half hour by car. Too far to walk. You want to go? See iguanas, crocodiles, *serpientes*. You want me to arrange trip, maybe tomorrow, maybe next day?"

Sheila scowls, grimaces, grits her teeth, and twitches in her seat, in desperation to emit signals. I avoid looking at her. All other eyes are on me. Juan Tonio.

Carlotta. Diego-Tattoos. Pedro. All are waiting for my response. Tension is obvious. My thoughts dart back and forth, like tennis players volleying, fiercely competing, battling for supremacy. Is he trying to pick me up? No, I'm too old. Get us out in the boonies? For what reason? Trying to be a good host?

"Yes, yes... I would like that. Just let us know when." The answer pops out, from deep within my heart, the same heart that has always been a touch too trusting. It is clear from the glances between Juan Tonio, Carlotta, Diego-Tattoos and Pedro that no one expects this response. Sheila holds her head in her hands, then downs her rum in one gulp and orders another.

I know I'm in trouble. I know what I've done. But hell, how can one go through life never taking a risk? Always suspecting the worst of people? Never really living?

"Esmerelda," Sheila admonishes, when we are later ensconced in our room. "What the hell were you thinking? Why did you agree to that? What if it is their intention to dump us in the lagoon? Who will ever find us?"

"Because... because... well, I prefer to give people the benefit of the doubt."

"Even when it's clear there is something really screwy going on here?"

"Yeah. I don't think these guys will hurt us. It seems to me they are just as suspicious of us as we are of them. If they are involved in something illegal and believe us to be 'infiltrators' or 'cops' they know we wouldn't go to a lagoon with them. I thought if we agreed, they would think of us as 'innocent tourists'. We are a helluva lot safer if they think we see nothing, hear nothing, know nothing. You saw how they looked when I said yes. They didn't expect that. So maybe this will be good for both of us. Maybe we can learn to trust each other. Besides we can email someone where we are going, and with whom."

"A lot of good that will do if we're buried in six feet of swamp muck. How about you go? And I stay here? At least there will be a witness at the murder trial."

"I wouldn't count on that. If they do me in, they'll get you too. We're in this together." In retrospect, that was not quite the right thing to say.

Actually, worrying about the lagoon tour was a waste of energy. For one reason or another, it was never again mentioned. To our relief, Sheila's in particular. If it was meant as a test, I passed. During the following week, however, several events occurred. I didn't interpret them as international-scale crises, as did Sheila. But I had to admit they were sufficiently serious to raise questions, imperil our friendship and Sheila's sanity.

One morning, over a bacon and scrambled eggs breakfast 'day', (which alternated with ham and cheese sandwich 'day') in stomps a thirtyish, heavy-set dark-haired, dark-skinned, dark-eyed hombre, built like a huge concrete block. He is dressed totally in black. Everything about him is black. Pedro mutters '*padrino*' under his breath, Carlotta vehemently nods, and both rush off to find Juan Tonio. Now, my Spanish is limited, but I know '*padrino*' means 'godfather'. Unfortunately, so does Sheila. To make matters worse, from his throat emerges the raspy voice of Marlon Brando who played the 'godfather' in the movie by the same name. Sheila suddenly loses her appetite, scuttles for cover like a bedbug in the spotlight. I hang around hoping to pick up some of the conversation, but it is hushed, and in Spanish that tumbles from their tongues like a rockslide down a slope.

Later that day, Pedro and Carlotta hound us to make a list of our favourite foods. I provide some ideas (that involve neither rice nor potatoes nor ham and cheese sandwiches) though it turns out that nothing we are served from that day forth even slightly resembles my suggestions.

Sheila proposes nil, convinced that they have decided to poison us instead of dumping us in the lagoon. When she develops severe stomach cramps one night, she insists she is dead right (excuse the pun). Subsequently, Sheila's meals consist primarily of *chifles* (pre-bagged platano chips) and pastries purchased at the corner store, washed down with cold cerveza or cheap rum.

The following day, we return from mid morning shopping, overloaded with a stash of Sheila's provisions. I open our bedroom door, motion for her to go in, and am withdrawing the key from the lock when she gasps. "Esmerelda," she shrieks, "look at this... just look at this." I am alarmed, thinking perhaps she has discovered a dead body. I gingerly step forward into the room, peer about, see nothing. "Now, maybe you will pay attention to what is going on here. Just look, look at this!" she screeches, sounding more panicked by the moment.

"Get a grip, Sheila," I see nothing. "What do you think you see?"

"I don't just think I see... I see! I see! I see!"

"What? What do you see?"

She points at the floor. Perhaps a spider? A centipede? A scorpion? Finally, I see what has her in such a state. A feather. A feather! A feather?

"He was in our room. Diego Tattoos. He always wears a feather. He had to be in our room. Check your passport. Check your money, credit cards. Jewellery. Medications." She is already rummaging through the closet where we have stashed our valuables.

"How do you know it's Diego-Tattoos's feather? Maybe it was on the maid's shoe or something."

"Look at it," she screeches. She streaks across the room, snatches it from the floor, whips around and waves it under my nose, as one might if one found the bullet that killed John Kennedy. "Just look at it. Oh yeah, it's his sure

48

enough. There are no birds around here with feathers like that. Use your head. Diego was in here. No question. And I sure don't trust him... do you know what is in his shoulder pack? When he opened it the other day I peered in. He has hundreds of condoms in there. What would he be doing with all those condoms?"

"Making love a lot?" I retort.

"Esmerelda, you are hopeless. Or stupid. He's probably pimping. Anyway, I am going straight to the owner. After I count my money and hide my passport. And if you are smart, you will do that too!"

"I don't have any jewellery worth stealing. And I forget how much cash I had. I have no idea if any is missing. But everything else seems to be here. And where do you suggest hiding it?"

"In your shoes. In your walking shoes. Under the sole inserts."

At dinner that night, Sheila confronts Juan Tonio. She sticks the feather under his nose. "Look at this," she demands. "A feather."

He turns toward me. Raises his eyebrows. I shrug my shoulders.

"Si. A feather. Where you get?" he asks her.

"In our room," she snaps. "Diego-Tattoos was in our room."

"Oh," he smiles. "Yes, he be there. The cleaning person say a light bulb is out, so I ask him to put in new one. He do. Ok now?"

She furrows her brow. Flicks the feather on the table in front of him. She does not believe him. He rolls his eyes at me. He does not understand her mistrust, her developing madness.

After that, several times each day, Sheila mentions checking out. Toward the end of the week, a plane buzzes the hotel. Twice. The owner and staff rush off without a word. We are alone in the hotel, except for Jorge's wife, Maria, who is cooking (if you can call it that) in the kitchen. Even Carlotta is absent. About an hour later Juan Tonio returns. Just before police cars begin to swarm the town. He appears concerned and quietly watches the street. I pretend to read. Sheila has her antennae up and can't sit still. She jiggles about and taps her foot, swings her head wildly in all directions as though she expects to be gunned down any second. Perhaps she isn't detective-material after all.

Another hour or so passes before the others return. All are grinning, speaking excitedly, slapping shoulders, and exchanging 'high fives'. That night, after we are in bed, they celebrate around the pool... with a small buffet and drinks for all. From our darkened room we hear clinking glasses, laughing, splashing, camaraderie. It is obvious they were successful in their mission, whatever that was. Perhaps better we don't know.

As we quietly watch from our room, Sheila whispers, "Well, I don't know what came down here today. Drug drop? Smuggling? Gun-running? Kidnapping? Robbery?"

"Who knows? They didn't involve us. See nothing, hear nothing, know nothing." But I see her trembling. I hear the tension in her voice. I understand she can no longer be pacified. Besides, I, too, finally accept something is off kilter.

"Esmerelda, without doubt they did something illegal, or immoral. Or both. And I saw machine guns in the back office when Juan Tonio slipped in the other day. Real machine guns! Can you believe that? AKA's or Uzis or whatever the hell they are called. Why would they have those? Who keeps those? I've had enough. I want out of here, with or without you."

"We are in South America," I say, "not in Canada. Things are different here. They have a hotel safe and inventory to protect, and police protection is less reliable than it is at home." But I knew if we stayed longer she'd crack, become a hopeless alcoholic, or leave without me and she is hardly in a state to look after herself. "Okay, in the morning I will tell Juan Tonio we are leaving. We can find a room in San Clemente or San Jacinto and make our plans for Esmeraldas from there. Okay?"

"Yes. Thank you." With tears in her eyes, she pours herself the last rum from the bottle, and we touch glasses.

As I fall asleep, I think about how our roles have changed. I have always seen her as the serious, steady one, considered myself the 'flake'. Yet here we are and, for this moment at least, I have the responsibility of moving us ahead, of finding a place where she feels safe. Sometimes in life we are challenged to do more than we ever believed we could. Sometimes we have no choice but to rise to the occasion.

The next morning I corner Juan Tonio. After exchanging usual pleasantries, I eye him directly. "We want to leave tomorrow. My friend is having a difficult time and wants to go to San Clemente or San Jacinto for a few days before we go to Esmeraldas."

He is silent a moment. Looks downward. At his pointed-outward duck toes encased in kid leather. He meets my gaze, his eyes soft, and nods. "Yes. I understand. I recommend hotel in San Jacinto. Is clean and very nice. Not so expensive as others and near the beach, which you like. Owner is friend. I make reservation for you. I arrange a driver to take you." He hesitates. "If you want," he adds. He does understand. He knows. And I know he knows. And he knows I know. What we both know, however, remains unspoken.

"Yes. I want. *Por favor*." I will not tell Sheila that Juan Tonio recommended the hotel and hired our driver.

"Ok. I tell them you come tomorrow." He grins. "You both want to go to Esmeraldas?"

"Yes. Please tell us the best way to get there."

"You sure? Two *mujeres*? *Senoras*? Sheila bad at travel. You sure you want to go? Maybe need escort? Esmeraldas close to Colombia border you know."

"Yes. We know. That is why I ask you the best way to go. No escort."

"Ok. I tell to you. You take bus to Bahia de Caraquez from San Jacinto. Cross the Chone River by boat to San Vicente. There you take bus or hire driver. From ferry lineup. Okay to trust them. Arrange price first. If you go by bus, go only during day. Stay away from beach at night. Stay in hotel when it be dark. I give you names of good hotels in the morning when you leave. You really want to go?"

"Yes. My name is Esmerelda. I want to go to Esmeraldas. Maybe named after me," I laugh. He grins, bobs his head like a marionette.

"Okay. I better pay our bill. I pass him my credit card."

"Oh, no," he says, "I no take credit card here. Only cash. We not set up for credit card."

"Oh, no," I reply. "We no have enough cash. We do dishes?" I tease him.

He chuckles. "No, you get cash. In Portoviejo. I send Tattoos with you."

"We can take a bus to Portoviejo today? What time? Sheila and I can go. We will be okay without an escort."

"Today, yes. Leave at 11:30. Tattoos go with you. He be good bodyguard," he beams. "He speak Spanish and he know where bank is. It be better for you." With that, he summons Tattoos, jabbers some Spanish. Tattoos looks at me, nods, smiles.

Juan Tonio continues, "He go with you. You come here at 11 hours, and walk to bus stop with Tattoos. Bring card to get cash from machine."

"Ok. See you then." Now I have the task of telling Sheila we are off to Portoviejo with Diego-Tattoos, whom she doesn't trust. But then, neither does she trust any of the others. No way will she stay here alone with them, so what the hell else do I do?

Off we go. Sheila is shaking either from nervousness or alcohol withdrawal, or both. Tattoos is calm, cool, confident. He struts along, glancing left and right as we move to the bus stop, the bag of condoms on his shoulder, his hand near the bulge on his hip. And I follow, trusting this will work. If I have even an ounce of skepticism, I dare not acknowledge it. What choice is there really?

The trip to Portoviejo is without event, except for us 'gringos', a novelty to bus passengers who smile and nod in welcome. Ecuadorians appreciate North Americans who try to communicate, to relate and to adapt to 'what is' rather than trying to change the culture. Tattoos-Diego swaggers aboard and finds us the best available seats. The bus is crowded, hot and muggy. It smells of perfume, perspiration and urine, with an occasional whiff of poopy diapers. We welcome whipping wind in through opened windows. Hairdos become irrelevant. Conversation is difficult above the volume of the music that varies from deafening to irritating to enjoyable, depending upon the individual taste of the driver, and the amount of hearing loss he seems to have incurred.

I concentrate on the passing landscape, cornfields, banana and pineapple plantations, rice paddies, small towns with weather-worn buildings, backyard pigs, painted roosters colourful fruit stands, leather-lined faces, and laughing children. Like Mexican men, fathers seem proud, caring, compassionate, in love with their children as much as, or maybe more than mothers, who have the daily chore of parenting.

Periodically the bus stops, drops off or picks up passengers, provides opportunity to purchase water, coconut milk or other drinks from outstretched hands lined up along the roadside. Sometimes it collects freight (baby strollers, boat motors, lawn chairs, the occasional crated chicken) only to drop items at seemingly unmarked driveways miles down the road. How do they know the correct destination? Periodically, individuals briefly enter the bus, offer ice cream or gum or candy or warm pastries from cloth-covered wicker baskets, and exit at the next stop. To transport themselves between the two places, they obviously have mastered the timing, hop on the next returning bus, and travel back and forth throughout the day.

Portoviejo, although without incident, is slightly less comforting. Tattoos hails a cab, spits instructions to the driver, none of which I understand, and motions us forward. We speed in and out of traffic as though we have a medical emergency, similar to an ambulance without the siren. I'm thinking that, at this rate, the probabilities of soon needing one with a siren are pretty high.

At the cash machine, we dutifully pass our cards to Diego. He punches in the appropriate information, though he lets us enter the PIN numbers, first from one of my cards, then from Sheila's. Her card is refused. We troop into the bank, where he consults a bank teller, shakes his head, tells us her card is not considered 'honourable' in this bank. Maybe another would work, maybe not, probably not.

"Sheila, do you have another card stashed in your shoes?"

"No, she shakes her head. I have some traveller's cheques though."

"They usually aren't accepted in Ecuador. Did I not tell you that before we left?"

"Esmerelda, you absolutely **did not**. You probably forgot to tell me... just like you forgot to..." She hesitates, glares at me, passes her hand over her forehead, and covers her eyes. As though she wants to disappear, find refuge in some unseen corner of her being.

"Never mind," I pacify, "I will get cash with my second card, enough for both of us." I untie my boot, haul a second card from beneath the insole.

"Now Diego-Tattoos will know where we keep our valuables," Sheila groans.

I am silent. My tongue hurts from biting it.

Tattoos returns our cards, pockets the cash and receipts, and hails another cab that whips us to the bus depot. To say Sheila is uneasy is an understatement. We have neither cash nor receipts. And I have taken out enough money to pay our hotel bills, in both Crucita and San Jacinto, and to get us to Esmeraldas and back. Just in case her card won't work in Bahia or Esmeraldas, or in event there are other hotels that refuse credit cards. So Diego is carrying a wad. Even I am a little nervous about this.

The crises occurs halfway back to Crucita. Sheila and I share a seat. Tattoos, slumped in his seat across the aisle, has nodded off. The bus brakes... at a roadblock of some sort. A huge truck is horizontal across the road, traffic is backed up, and people are milling around.

"I've read about this sort of thing," Sheila stutters under her breath. "They stop buses, pull people off, rob them blind... money, credit cards, passports, jewellery. In some cases, they even shoot them on the spot and leave them for dead on the highway."

I'm not sure what I should say to her. I know what she says is possible. But these occurrences are uncommon in Ecuador, especially in daylight, on a main road. I say nothing.

"Maybe it was all planned from the hotel. Maybe that is why Juan Tonio sent Diego-Tattoos with us… maybe they are in on it. Maybe that's what they were doing the other day, when they had the party. Maybe they robbed a bus."

"Shhh," I motion. "Calm down. I'll wake Tattoos."

I poke him in the ribs. *"Qué pasa?* What happens?" I ask.

He shoots upward, jerks around, bewildered, as though for a moment he is trying to get his bearings. You know, it is that confusion that sometimes occurs between sleeping and waking, as one moves from one level of consciousness to another. He leaps to his feet, and shouts to the driver, who promptly answers. Words are loudly exchanged. Passengers crane necks and jabber to each other. I understand nothing. Sheila perceives only that we are about to be murdered.

Diego turns to me, motions us to stay in our seats. *"Accidente.* It be ok. No worry," he consoles. "We go soon." He leans over, pats my hand. This tattooed brute smiles broadly and pats my hand. Hell, if we are going down, it is not without empathy. Or reassurance. Or comfort. This gives new meaning to 'killing with kindness', I think.

I relay the information to Sheila, for all the good it does. She is as tense as a stretched slingshot. She fails to relax, even when the police arrive, the debris is cleared, and we are once again on our way, even when we are back at the hotel and she is secure in her room. To her 'safe' is relative. Only after a couple of double-rums does she unwind.

I try to explain that if they wanted to rob or kill us, they would have done so by now. After all, did they not return our cards and cash the minute we were back in the hotel? But she isn't buying. Hell, at this point, she is incapable of hearing, of rational thinking. We definitely need a discussion on whether or not she is really prepared for our jaunt to Esmeraldas, or whether we should be seeking a psych ward or detoxification center instead. I will put it to her straight. If we are to go, she is going to have to draw on resources I have thus far not seen. However, I will wait until we get to San Jacinto.

Part Three: Respite

Our stay in San Jacinto is heaven. The hotel is walled, with an inner courtyard, gorgeous kidney-shaped swimming pool, Jacuzzis and a sauna. Spanish and English-speaking staff members are welcoming and intent on pleasing. The cook is fabulous, a real 'foodie' if not a gourmet. Nearby small shop vendors are friendly. There are a few ex-pats, with whom one can share a beer and chat about news from 'home'. Best of all, Sheila feels protected, safe. She believes we have escaped the Mafioso. I do not mention Juan Tonio's connection with this hotel owner.

Each morning we stroll the beaches and watch the fishermen haul in their catch. I am mesmerized by lines of short, stocky Ecuadorians with bulging biceps and sinewy calves, attired in brightly coloured shorts and tee shirts, digging bare feet into the sand as they strain under the weight of hand-pulled nets. Sometimes nets yield little, other times they are bursting. One morning the catch is forty-five tons of fish. The beach bustles with ice-filled trucks and fishermen and villagers. What appeals to me most, however, is not the size of the catch, but the cooperative nature of it all. Yes, boat owners and truckers seem to get the best of the catch, but it seems everyone who helps is entitled to some fish. Even seven and eight-year-olds who carry pails or ropes are given a share. I hope the incredible community spirit around an industry that has sustained village inhabitants for generations is never lost to commercial interests.

The fishermen seem equally intrigued with the interest shown by the pale-skinned '*gringa*' in what to them must be routine. In time, a few approach and exchange pleasantries, or wave from their vehicles as they pass by. I am encouraged to examine species; they teach me names and identifying characteristics. One day they point out what looks like a miniature stingray and demonstrate how to 'pop' a fully formed baby from its dead mother's pregnant belly. Perhaps this is meant as a test of fortitude or endurance. The following day one of the men either offers me a job or proposes marriage. I am uncertain which. Until my Spanish improves it is best to agree to nothing.

After a week or so, when Sheila has regained her composure, confidence and sense of humour (as well as a measure of sobriety), she swears she is up to an 'Esmeraldas' adventure and promises to 'go with the flow' of travelling in another country. Thus we firm up our plans. I have secreted away the names of the hotels recommended by Juan Tonio, and check them on the internet. All appear to be good choices. I pay online for the first night in Bahia de Caraquez, and reserve a second night in Canoa. I decide, however, to not reveal the source of hotel recommendations.

We have a fantastic send-off. The mists of dawn dissipate to reveal a clear blue sky teased only by a bare rim of cloud on the far horizon. In mid-morning heat, with overstuffed backpacks, filled water bottles and petty cash in our pockets, we hop on the San Jacinto bus to Bahia. The fare is eighty cents, the trip about fifty minutes. The day is promising. Our spirits are high. We resolve to be daunted by nothing. Little do we know.

Bahia de Caraquez, a beautiful coastal city on the Pacific, has been reconstructed since its 1997-1998 devastation associated with Él Niño floods, earthquake and consequential mudslides. (Note: subsequent to writing this much of Bahia de Caraquez along with coastal areas both north and south were severely damaged in the earthquake of April, 2016.)

We hail one of the 'bipeds', as I unofficially call them. Carts for two people are attached to a single bicycle, propelled by a solitary muscular-calved driver who pedals anywhere in the city, with the fervour of someone escaping execution, for the equivalent of fifty cents to a dollar. Our hotel, a quaint older building, is constructed like a maze. After passing through several hallways, twists and turns, we reach our room, cozy but attractively furnished with cane and antique wood. A salt breeze wafts in through open shutters. Here, we will sleep like lambs or, as it turns out, more like lambs the eve of their slaughter.

The remainder of our time in Bahia is spent exploring the seaside market and tiny shops. An archaeological museum boasts pottery from the Valdivia culture, one of the oldest settlements recorded in America (3500-1800 BC), theorized to have a past connection with the Jamon culture in Kyushu, Japan. Rum-infused drinks and sumptuous langostino (huge prawns or tiny lobsters) grilled in butter with garlic and lime, at the Puerto Amistad Yacht Club, crown an enjoyable day. At my insistence, as advised by Juan Tonio, we return to our hotel at dusk, and join other 'gringos' at the bar for a nightcap. Sheila is content. All is well.

After a leisurely brunch of juice, coffee, cheese, fresh fruit and an omelet stuffed with tomatoes, onions, and peppers the following morning, we set off for the ferry. A short wait and thirty-five cents later we are assisted aboard a dilapidated motorized panga, a boat that carries about two dozen people across the Chone River to San Vicente. We are just casting off when Sheila erupts, "We have no life jackets. Look. Everyone in the other boats has life jackets. Where are ours? Why do we have none? Are we on an authentic boat?"

"Well," I reply, "since we are moving on top of the water, I believe this is an authentic boat. I don't know why we have no life jackets. But it is too late to get them now. There is little wind. The water is relatively calm. We should be fine. That is, providing you don't panic and tip the boat."

"You know," Sheila says, "whenever I hear stories about ferries going down off the coast of Taiwan or Korea or China, all those people without life jackets, all those people who drowned, I always say *God, were they stupid. I would never get on a boat without a life jacket.* Yet here I am."

I try to calm her. "This boat goes back and forth all the time. Look around. No one else seems concerned. We'll be okay. Right?"

No sooner are the words out of my mouth the watercraft's engine sputters and spits, chokes out one final breath, dies. Several attempts to start it fail. We are floating about, rocked by the waves of other boats passing by.

"Oh lord," Sheila implores, "here we go... I just knew it. Had a sense, I did."

"Well, you know, Sheila, they... your psychics and spirit guides and gurus... they all say that one invites an experience. Don't they? Might you have invited this one?"

She is quiet. Contemplating.

The boat motor stutters, burps, catches. We are in business. Maybe Sheila has powers of which I am unaware. We begin to move a few feet forward. The engine dies again. More sputters and snorts. The boat operator utters a few words beneath his breath. I have no idea if they are curses or prayers. Whatever, we are going nowhere quickly.

Someone pulls out a cell phone, calls for help. By now, some minutes later, we are beginning to rock. The sky has greyed. The wind has come up, along with the waves. Water splashes into the boat. Someone begins bailing. We huddle together, pull out our rain jackets, tuck them around our shuddering shoulders. I know we are too far from shore to make it swimming in a current like this. I am beginning to think perhaps Sheila is right. I am beginning to wish I had my Mexican rosary beads. I am beginning to think I should have finalized my will before I left home.

The boat is silent, but for the slapping of waves, a wailing baby, a few grumbling voices, and the guy on the cell phone pleading in desperation. The boat crew exchange animated suggestions or displeasures... I mean who knows? I suppose genuine Spanish speakers know. But, as Sheila reminds me, without my dictionary we have no recourse but to wait, no choice but to be 'present in the moment.' For the second time this trip, I envision stuffing my absent dictionary down her very present throat.

An eternity later, which is likely not more than ten or fifteen minutes, a second panga pulls up alongside. Both operators exchange words and at first it seems passengers will have to make the transfer between rocking boats in waters becoming increasingly choppy. Not something I anticipate with utter joy. Not something Sheila will ever do without someone first rendering her unconscious. However, after some manipulation of boats, our craft is hooked up to the 'towboat', which chugs ahead, clearly labouring under its weight, slowly dragging us to shore. San Vicente, an industrialized, dowdy, untidy, grey fishing town, resembles Shangri-la.

By the time we disembark, the drizzle has stopped. Patches of blue are exposed between rapidly dispersing clouds, and the emerging bright, hot sun instantly transforms our surroundings into a humid jungle. Rivulets of perspiration replace raindrops that dried only moments ago. We have survived the storm. Or so we think. However, as is common in life… although one may win a battle or two, the war continues. One should not be fooled. This is a respite, one inviting us to a new experience. An awakening, as Sheila would say, one of which we are not yet aware.

Part Four: The Reckoning

"Let's replenish our water before we grab a taxi," I suggest. "We can get to Canoa (also severely damaged in 2016), catch a late lunch at the Bamboo Inn, and still have time to explore the town, or watch the surfers before sunset." The Bamboo Inn had been recommended not only by Juan Tonio, but also by a couple of ex-pats. "The best tequila prawns in the world", they said. "You gotta try them", they said. To be honest, the tequila prawns are my sole motivation for stopping in Canoa, although I have enticed Sheila with the promise of gorgeous, muscle-bound surfers.

"Why don't we rent a moped cart?" I ask. We have lots of time. The sun is shining. It won't be quite as fast as a taxi, but we will see more of the countryside. And enjoy some fresh air in the process."

"Sure, why not? This is an adventure, right?" She readily agrees. I almost faint.

Without hesitation, the first moped-cart driver in line nods and snatches the US five dollar bill we offer him. From the round of guffaws that follow, we conclude we have overpaid, even though a return trip to Canoa will require at least an hour and a half of his time plus gasoline. We don't mind. To us, this seems more than reasonable.

He motions us aboard and we are off, sitting side by side, facing the front. About fifteen minutes later the skies suddenly darken, open, spilling torrents of rain once more like the Asian monsoons. Our driver slows, reaches back, pulls down a plastic sheet to shelter us. Guess again. The sheet blows back and forth in the wind. We are soon soaked from waist down and shivering beneath our lightweight jackets. To make matters worse, water is splashing up from the road, splattering our bare legs with dirt and oil. When semi-trailers pass by, honest to god, we are in danger of drowning. I kid you not.

"Unbelievable," Sheila says, "bloody unbelievable. Guess we should have taken a taxi after all."

"How the hell was I to know?" I shoot back, slightly guilt-ridden by her underhanded criticism, "twenty minutes ago the sun was shining."

"Maybe those moped drivers knew. Maybe that's why they were laughing their fool heads off. Maybe we should turn back."

"Well, we cannot get much wetter. And we are likely almost half way there. We can have a hot shower at the hotel. And if you think we are wet, just look at the driver." I am determined not to miss those tequila prawns.

"Are you sure? Many South American hotels have no hot water."

"The Bamboo Inn does. Juan..." I bite my tongue, "I checked it out."

"Good. I'm looking forward to it."

She has missed the reference... thank heavens.

63

Suddenly, the moped engine misses, chokes, sputters, dies.

"Probably wet," I offer. "Maybe that's why the guys were laughing their heads off."

After ten or fifteen minutes, the driver manages to get it started and we are off again. The monsoon has failed to let up.

Although it could have been one of several reasons, we never did find out for certain what spawned the guffaws from the moped drivers. Hell, before we reached Canoa, the moped stalled three more times, and twice discarded its chain. What should have been a forty-five minute ride or, an hour at most, stretched into more than three hours.

We asked to be dropped off at the Bamboo Inn near the beach. Just as the moped took what was in all likelihood its last breath, the driver motioned toward a beach restaurant constructed of bamboo. I suppose he figured his guess was good as any. Or he knew we weren't going any further. I strongly suspected it wasn't the right place, but welcomed shelter from the pouring rain. Besides, that we would be well received in any decent establishment was unlikely. We looked like two water retrievers that had frolicked along a muddy shoreline. At least here, they wouldn't mind our dripping onto the sand floor. At least here was a bathroom, albeit a decrepit one. And hot coffee. And the best ham and cheese sandwich I have ever eaten.

An hour or so later, the rain has let up. The moped has been dragged away. We decide to find our hotel. We pool our pocket money to pay the bill, count it up.

"We're short about four dollars," says Sheila, "you'll have to dig into your stash."

My heart leaps into my brain, just before it sinks to my toes like a rock in a pond. I feel my face drain of blood. I struggle for words. "Hhh, hh, holy hell, I don't have my stash. Hell, I have no money. No credit cards. Nada."

Sheila gasps, chokes on her words. "Esmerelda... what... how... oh my god, you forgot, you forgot again... where? How could you forget?" She groans, rolls her head from side to side like a stoned marionette.

"They're in my shoes, Sheila, in my boots, under the insole, where you insisted I keep them. Only it was so hot I wore my sandals. I left the others in our room in San Jacinto."

"Oh, lord, what do we do now?"

"Pray?" I thought of the bus ride to Armeria a few years previous. "Got any rosary beads?"

"No, but maybe they'd take a tee shirt in trade for the four bucks?"

"Maybe, or maybe not. Why don't we first find out if your credit card works. You did bring your card?"

"Yep. Got mine. In my bra."

"Well, why the hell didn't you try to get cash in Bahia?"

"Because I thought you had yours."

"Okay. You stay here and I'll find the hotel. Give me your card... they won't know I'm not you, and I made the reservation. We have to pay for the room anyway. Maybe they can give us a few bucks extra. Or tell me where I might get cash with this? What's your password? Did you bring your travellers' cheques?"

"Of course not," Sheila snapped, "you told me nobody takes them here." She pulls her credit card from under her shirt and hands it over, whispers her password.

I nod. Turn to the young couple behind the counter. "*Necesito mas dinero*," I tell them. I need more money. He nods, she smiles; they know from our voices something is amiss. I leave Sheila there as the guarantee I will return. Though in retrospect I must admit there were moments I actually considered other alternatives.

I return an hour or so later, just as the skies reopen. Sheila looks hopeful until I shake my head. I have found no one that will accept her credit card, including the actual Bamboo Inn where we are to stay, or rather were to stay. Back to square one.

So here we are, sitting with our heads in our hands, wondering how the hell to get out of this mess. We consider options. Maybe we can borrow a few bucks from one of the surfers on the beach, or from shopkeepers. Maybe we should look for a tourist who speaks English and will hopefully understand our predicament. The problem is we have to catch a bus or ride back to Bahia, or perhaps San Jacinto, before we can access cash, and we cannot do that until tomorrow. Maybe we should find the police station.

Though, since I already have a reputation with the Mexican police, I am hesitant to establish one with Ecuadorian's finest.

"*Hola, señoras, como estas*? How you do?" chants a familiar voice from behind me.

Once again, Sheila is frozen in her seat, her mouth open like a fish sucking air. Just before she mutters, "Holy hell." I twist my neck. It's Juan Tonio and Jorge, his security guard.

I turn back toward Sheila, whisper, "You always say prayers are answered in the strangest ways."

"Oh, lord, yes... yes ma'am, you got that right," she replies.

"*Hola!*" I stand up. Good to see you."

"*Si*. You too." Juan Tonio is grinning. "I hear some señoras in town need help. *Dinero*. Money?" He has a way of dispensing with the unnecessary, cutting to the core of the apple, one might say. And in this moment, I love him. I love him for who he is. I realize it is no accident he is standing before us now.

"I pay your bill. You come with me. I pay your hotel, your room. We stay too. In another room," he quickly adds. "We go to Esmeraldas tomorrow. You pay me money back in San Jacinto. Come. We talk."

"What the f...," Sheila sputters, "how the f... did he find us?

"Enough," I say, holding my hand up like a traffic cop, "enough. These guys want to help us. We are in desperate need of help. Enough already. Learn to recognize an angel when you see one."

"Angel?" she dares.

I glare. She shuts up. Juan Tonio and Jorge, grinning like lottery winners, pay our bill, pick up our backpacks, and lead us to the Bamboo Inn.

Later, after our room is secured for the night, after hot showers and clean clothes, we are treated to drinks and dinner, the elusive out-of-this-world tequila prawns. Since Jorge speaks no English but smiles a lot, and since Sheila is reticent to speak but frowns a lot, the conversation is pretty much between Juan Tonio and I.

"So how did you find us?"

"I know. I check with hotels in San Jacinto. (He doesn't betray me.) One owner say you leave for Esmeraldas yesterday. He say you stay in Bahia de Caraquez, then go to Canoa. I need to pick up auto part at Colombia border, so I go. Jorge come with me. Tattoos is hopeless. He carry gun but no can shoot it. He too soft. So Jorge come. Never go to Colombia border without guns."

"Guns? You have guns?"

"*Si*. Machine guns. *Son necesarios*. Not often dangerous here. But maybe one day it is; if you carry big enough gun you not need to ever shoot it."

"How did you know we were here at the restaurant?"

His eyes twinkle. I ask at hotel. They say a gringo señora had no money to pay for room. I ask around. Many others say same thing, show where you go."

"Why important for you to find us?" I am now beginning to speak his English, since my Spanish doesn't quite make the grade.

"Oh... oh," he says, "I worry. In Colombia we respect señoras. *Muchas,* very much. They are mothers, sisters, tias, how you say, aunties. We look... we look out for them. I worry. You not have good Spanish. *No muy bien.* You say to me one hot day, you wave your paper before your face, you say *muy caliente.* That mean 'hot woman'. *Necesitas,* you need to say *hace calor* if you talk about *temperatura.* Another time you say *embarazada*; that mean you have baby in stomach. So I worry."

"My Spanish that bad?" I laugh.

"*Si*," he nods, chuckles, hesitates. Continues. "Another time you want *pollo asado,* chicken roasted, you ask for *polla asado.* That be male part, how you say? Penis roasted? Yes, I worry. I worry. You meet bad people. Get in trouble."

"And so we did." I laugh.

"Because of you," Sheila snarls, "not because of bad Spanish or bad people."

I glower. I've had enough. Juan Tonio misses nothing.

"And you Señora Sheila," he turns toward her "I worry about you too. Esmerelda try to make this good trip for you. You need to open eyes, see South America. Ecuador is beautiful country. Most people good people. But is not same as North America. You want Holiday Inn? Better to go home. You need to make trip good for you. Esmerelda not can do that for you."

Sheila is quiet for some time before she attempts to join the conversation. Juan Tonio translates and includes Jorge. We laugh about our 'body guard' Tattoos falling asleep on the bus from Portoviejo. We learn that he distributes condoms (which are difficult to access in a rural Catholic country) to pharmacies and stores in smaller towns, in cooperation with public health authorities. The phoenix is his 'mascot', the feather its symbol, because he is trying to recreate himself subsequent to turbulent teen years. We discover that Juan Tonio had us followed in Crucita for our 'protection' until we became acclimatized (although he did admit he had been warned by Ecuador Immigration authorities that Sheila, from Tree Frog Island, was considered a suspicious person).

One by one the 'oddities' are explained. Carlotta asked so many questions because she hoped one day to go to Canada. Pedro was amazed at the very possibility policewomen might ride motorcycles. The lagoon trip was cancelled because of Sheila's obvious fear. *Padrinos* and *madrinos* (godfathers and godmothers) are chosen not only at baptism but also at high school graduation.

We never learn, however, what occurred the day the planes buzzed the hotel and all staff disappeared only to return hours later in a euphoric state. Sometimes, some questions are best left unasked.

After that night Sheila undergoes a transformation. Unbelievably so. She becomes more Esmerelda than I am. It's like a demon has been unleashed. She is wild about the motorcycle, thrilled by speed, delighted with the wind in her hair. She pleads with Jorge to go faster. She suggests stopping to eat at quaint little shacks on white sand beaches, without questioning whether or not she'll get food poisoning. She listens for birdsong in verdant tropical rainforests, photographs cattle ranches, and pees in the bushes. She actually begs to shoot the machine gun and is really ticked when Juan Tonio and Jorge refuse.

Three days later we were escorted back to San Jacinto. Our trip to Esmeraldas was successful. True, we found no emeralds. But we struck pure gold. We made two new friends, two Colombian gentlemen... or two of Tony Soprano's 'boys'. It depends on one's perspective I suppose. In the end, it didn't really matter.

LIZZIE'S DEBUT

"Let your smile change the world but don't let the world change your smile."

Author Unknown

I swear to this day that the Galapagos land iguana on Isabela Island smiled at me, I mean really smiled. He was a magnificent, handsome, affable golden-scaled creature, shaded with tangerine, indigo, coffee, crimson and amethyst, one who obviously preferred basking in attention to lazing in midday sun. As I crouched before him, crooning sweet nothings and focusing my camera, he rose on his short, stubby legs, curiously ambled forward, at about the same speed as the flow of molasses in a Canadian prairie winter, fixed his gaze upon me and smiled, in fact gleefully grinned. I questioned, aware of my advancing age, whether in fact he noted some resemblance to his species. No matter. He beamed. I swear it.

At that moment I was reminded of another iguana with whom I had become acquainted some years earlier on Sint Eustatius. Lizzie was a regular patron of the Mill House, an unobtrusive, Caribbean-styled, rattan-furnished beach hotel sporting a first-rate open-air restaurant. I would think that Lizzie was a Lesser Antillean iguana, except that, measuring about two and a half feet from nose to tail tip, 'she' seemed larger than she should have been for the species. With mammoth scales down her metallic charcoal back, spikes adorning her spine, tubercles gracing her face and an armoured leather-like fold hanging from her chin, she had been denied the multi-hued splendour of her Galapagos relative. In fact, I have since concluded, based on her size and colour, that Lizzie was a male. It just makes

71

sense. After all, we do know, having seen cross-dressers, that what is sometimes perceived as a rather unattractive overweight female can indeed be a very handsome, rotund male in drag.

What Lizzie lacked in beauty, 'she' made up for in her shy, gentle demeanour. In spite of her apparent timidity and need for solitude, she daily frequented the restaurant, usually around lunch hour. Seemed to me that was more a scheduled event than it was a coincidence. Descending a palm frond, she crept, or sometimes plopped, onto her perch atop one of several thatched umbrella-shaped roofs shading circular tables. There she remained motionless for inordinate periods of time, inert, lusting after a slice of juicy papaya or a centerpiece flower bud. She was docile, so unassuming that none of the diners, no one, no one except those of us privy to the hotel's deeper secrets, knew Lizzie lounged overhead. That, however, as we later learned, was to change, and not for the better.

Lunch on the terrace overlooking the turquoise sea was an occasion in itself. Morley, one of the owners, usually poised, business-like, was a superb gourmet chef who turned out, among other mouth-watering delights, the most scrumptious conch chowder ever. Furthermore, the diverse cast of characters, varying somewhat on a daily basis, never failed to be fascinating, intriguing, entertaining. Unique bordering on unusual, possibly even bizarre. My kind of people, possibly blood relatives. (I use the genetic card whenever possible... it tends to excuse many idiosyncrasies.)

From a combination of islanders, hotel guests, tourists, entrepreneurs, bureaucrats or professionals, one could pick up local gossip, travel tips, political viewpoints, world news, or perhaps a lover if that was your desire and you were travelling alone, although being alone was not necessarily a prerequisite. Furthermore, for those of us whose most serious decision of the day was what to choose for lunch, it had become an amusement, a Russian roulette-like game, to guess who would be under the umbrella upon which Lizzie sprawled.

This day, my companion and I arrive shortly before noon, as is our custom. Hunched at the bar, where he has been since morning, is Sam, an over-the-hill retired librarian, rather bland in appearance, nondescript, short, stocky, caramel-skinned, brown-haired, attired in tan shorts and shirt, one of those people no one really notices. Unfortunately, it takes several Heinekens before his love of life, sense of humour, active mind and appreciation of the natural world become apparent.

Parked at the other end of the bar is a corpulent forties-something male, inappropriately suited in expensive, grey pinstriped wool partially obscuring his protruding belly. He has slicked-back salt and pepper hair, spectacles perched on the end of his hawk-like nose, cigarette dangling from browned stubby fingers. Rivulets of perspiration trickle, drip from his brow down his face, dampening his collar and shirt front. He sits apart, his back slightly turned, as though afraid he will catch something contagious, and continues his chain smoking throughout a three-martini lunch.

We choose our usual corner table, an ideal vantage point from which to view the entire patio. In an instant, our waiter, Jimmy, a slim, amiable, efficient, jovial young Statian, impeccable in black pants and white shirt with open collar, is beside us, pouring coffee. He knows us well.

"Who's the guy in the suit?" I whisper.

Under his breath, Jimmy murmurs, "A lawyer from Sint Maarten. He's representing a client here. You know Humphrey something-or-other Jones, that filthy rich off-island guy that owns most of the hillside? Well, he's suing Obediah, his neighbour."

"What for?"

"For allowing his chickens to recklessly wander."

"But Obediah has no money does he?"

"None. They'll likely try to take his land."

I ponder this for a moment, realize that I really know nothing about this island and these islanders and their friends and adversaries and burdens.

In a second corner, over bowls of steaming curried goat, a freckled, sandy-haired medical equipment salesman, with rolled up shirt sleeves, open collar and unknotted tie, 'pitches' his client. She, the clinic administrator, a serious, matronly, prim, flat-chested middle-aged woman, with her graying hair confined in a tight knot at the nape of her neck, listens attentively, nodding and bobbing, as a marionette might, struggling to get a word in edgewise. She is all about business.

Tending bar is Tom, blacker than a coal bin with a grin like the Cheshire cat. One can see the whites of his eyes from fifty paces, maybe more. Although he was suave, stocky, trim when we first met him, he has become slightly pot-bellied with time. Tom, genial, good-humoured and a bit of a prankster, gets a kick out of lacing my Pina Colada with extra rum, simply to determine, I believe, how quickly he can get me tipsy. Or maybe he just likes us as much as we do him. One year when we were unable to make the trip, he sent to Canada, via an acquaintance, a delectable rum cake made by his mother. It was pierced with holes, no doubt for the purpose of adding another several shots of rum. My speech slurred after one piece. It was definitely the best rum cake I have ever tasted... or shall I say absorbed?

Many times Tom has promised or threatened, depending how one views the situation, to invite us to his mother's house after a successful iguana hunt. I live in fear that he will. I have no idea what I'd do. How does one insult the hostess by refusing to eat the special dish she prepares? Worse yet, what if one manages to swallow it but it refuses to stay there?

I've already had a previous experience of this sort, in a restaurant no less, after I indulged in several selections from the buffet table. At the very moment I discovered I had eaten rabbit, I was reminded of Peanut, the wild baby rabbit I rescued from sure death, fed with an eyedropper for many nights until he flourished and became an engaging pet. At that very instant my dinner exited more quickly than it entered as I made a mad dash for the washroom.

Fortunately, we never received Tom's invitation and, because we didn't, I instinctively knew Lizzie was safe. Over the years, in fact, I concluded that Tom had always been pulling my leg, bluffing, delighting in my reaction, accurately gauging my breathless silence, clenched teeth, whitened knuckles that appeared at first mention of iguana stew. Considering the speed at which iguanas usually move, he simply could not have been that lousy a hunter.

Now, as we savour the daily special, grilled lime snapper with coconut rice-stuffed red peppers, we scrutinize other restaurant patrons, who saunter in a few at a time.

Off to one side, a female realtor, casually attired in cobalt screen-printed pants and loose white shirt, animatedly discusses properties with her obviously affluent, heavily- jeweled, extravagantly but formally-clothed clients, now perspiring beneath their wool serge. They are probably in their seventies, speak heavily accented English and take copious notes throughout the meal.

Dominating the room is a balding, loud-mouthed, overweight and overbearing Tony Soprano-like American tourist, wearing a tropical green, white and red hibiscus printed shirt, with an enormous cigar thrusting from its pocket.

He stops at a table. "Sit here," he orders. His wife, placid, doe-eyed, raven-haired, statuesque and sophisticated in black silk, sits.

"I'll order," he declares. "You never get it right". She doesn't reply. "I'll get you a salad. Wouldn't hurt you to lose a pound or two". She nods, says nothing.

Subsequently, guzzling several bourbon-on-the-rocks, devouring a couple of burgers and fries, he continues to berate, belittle and bully his wife, as he did the previous evening. She, eyes downcast, sips a gin and tonic and, rather like a sandpiper, silently picks away at her Caesar salad.

At the edge of the patio facing the sea, their backs to the room, young honeymooners, barefooted, with matching light denim shirts thrown loosely over their swimwear, huddle, shoulders touching, noses inches apart. They seldom converse but gaze into their partner's eyes as might a dumb struck deer caught in the headlights, occasionally caress or kiss, undisturbed by the waiter bringing bowls of gazpacho that they subsequently spoon-feed to each other. Almost makes me wish I were back at that stage of romance.

Last to arrive are four 'little old ladies', all with various shades of blue or mauve-tinted hair, all with rounded rouged cheeks, cupid-bowed mouths, all shaped more or less like Santa or Mrs. Claus, all in variously-hued, pastel miniature floral prints stretched tautly across ample, sagging breasts. They are obviously celebrating one of their birthdays, with much enthusiasm, exhilarated chatter and infectious laughter. I'm aware that the fact one has reached another birthday at this point in life may, in itself, be cause for such jubilation. Before they tackle their lobster salad chock-full of red pepper, avocado and slices of succulent mango, garnished with golden and blood red nasturtiums, they toast the 'birthday girl', clinking frozen pink daiquiris that Tom has attentively prepared.

Just as Sam, now sufficiently satiated and sedate, slides off his stool, slightly staggers before he steadies himself, then turns to leave, it happens. In the snap of a finger, yet seemingly in slow motion. The brief crack of splitting bamboo. Splat. Lizzie smacks the table below. Audible silence, for just a fraction of a second. A moment frozen in time. An instant before all hell breaks loose. Utter pandemonium. Sort of like an explosion, I would think.

Dishes shatter. Cutlery flies. Glasses smash. Ice cubes roll like dice. Pink liquid spills across white linen, spreads like ink on a blotter, like a rampant virus infecting everyone it touches. Food splatters everywhere. Four no-longer-joyfully-celebrating ladies simultaneously leap to their feet, chairs clattering to the floor. They shriek and wail, as though their fingernails had been involuntarily extracted. Sweeping chunks of lobster and juicy mango from their breasts, brushing gobs of avocado from their cheeks, picking nasturtiums from their blue and lavender hair, they charge from the terrace, like raging bulls through the streets of Pamplona.

The lawyer is the first to react. He races after the women, hurling business cards on our tables as he whizzes by, "If any of you are interested in suing..."

Morley, in chef's apron, bursts from the kitchen, glances about, retreats, returns and dashes across the room clutching a bottle of champagne, pursues the lawyer and the fleeing women. However, it is too late. He suspects, perhaps even hopes and prays that he, nor any of us, will ever see them again. Particularly not in a courtroom. He withdraws to the kitchen, the champagne under his arm. Shortly thereafter, we hear the cork pop.

Reactions from other patrons vary. Jimmy, well familiarized with iguanas and Lizzie, scrutinizes the entire scene, shakes his head and without batting an eye, grabs a broom and bucket, gathers up broken glass and chunks of debris from the flagstone. One wonders if this has happened before.

Sam whoops, "Wow! I'll be damned! Woo-Hoo! Yeah! YEAH!! Way to go, Lizzie! One for the critters!"

The clinic administrator meticulously folds her napkin, unfolds herself, announces that she must prepare staff for potential cardiac arrest patients, stalks out. The salesman, tossing some bills on the table and mumbling something about the necessity for more resuscitator units, scurries after her.

The potential property owners gasp in shock, choke, "You no tell uzz there ver repteelses on theezz eezland. Repteels! You ecxpectz uzz buy propertees vith repteels? Nah, vee vill findz un-nudder eezland. Vun vithout repteels."

At this, the realtor, also throwing bills on the table, speeds after them imploring "Wait, wait. Iguanas are not dangerous. This reptile is harmless. Stop! Come back!" Her shouting soon fades to muttering, "Galloping goats! This was a sure deal. This deal could have got me a car... and a few cows... another donkey... several goats... and..."

'Tony' leaps to his feet, waves his fists, vociferously curses and berates the management for carelessness and stupidity. Tony's wife, composed, pauses briefly, purposefully rises from her chair and, staring at her husband, coldly and solemnly commands, "For godsake, shut up. For the first time in your life, just shut up!" She turns on her heel and sweeps from the room, her elegance intact. He flings down some bills, downs his bourbon, docilely follows.

I silently, or not so silently, I am no longer certain, cheer uninhibitedly.

Tom, who moves to assist Jimmy, grins, bares his ivories, and with a thumbs-up questions "Dinner at Mum's house? Tonight at six?" He winks.

The honeymooners remain completely oblivious and continue to spoon feed each other chocolate-sauced ice cream sundaes.

Lizzie, too, is oblivious to the chaos she has caused, the consequences of her debut, her impact on so many lives. Remaining on the table, aware of her good fortune, she is intently but placidly munching succulent mango chunks and nasturtiums. And she is smiling... I swear that Lizzie is smiling. As am I.

Subsequently, I have frequently wondered if we, too, as I suspect was the case with both iguanas, are unaware of our influence on those around us, are unmindful of the effect of a smile.

Sheila Carnegie

THE SNAKE THAT WASN'T

"Fear has its use, but cowardice has none. I may not put my hand into the jaws of a snake, but the very sight of the snake need not strike terror into me. The trouble is that we often die many times before death overtakes us."

Mahatma Ghandi

Daybreak, cotton-candy pink, crept over Sint Eustatius (Statia), from a hazy, azure horizon. I treasured early Caribbean mornings, cool, crisp air, gentle salt breezes, the tangerine, disc-like sun unfolding cerulean skies, fraught with promise of scorching heat. This day, my friend and I anticipated an early morning flight to Saba.

From Sint Maarten, we approached Saba's four hundred-meter airstrip, the world's shortest commercial runway, at least at that time, resembling a one-lane, paved road precariously perched on the side of a precipitous rocky coastline, sheer cliffs rising vertically from waters below. Then, several years ago, only Canadian Otters, and only pilots with a special 'ticket' over and above regular licenses, were allowed to land.

We dared not breathe as the plane touched down at one end of the runway and braked hard, slightly skidding to an abrupt stop at the other end. A dozen feet further and we would have plummeted into the indigo ocean beyond.

Stunned into silence, the fourteen of us aboard remained temporarily frozen in our seats. A blanched-faced passenger who had occupied the co-pilot's seat burst from the cockpit, perspiration dripping from his brow, "If you... if you th-thought it was bad back here, you... you... you sh-should have been up front!" he stuttered. "Anyone want to

81

join me at the nearest bar?" This remarkable landing, however, was neither to be the most memorable event of the day, nor the only reason for hitting the bar.

Saba, approximately five square miles in size, is the tiniest island and the highest point in the Netherlands Antilles. Visible from Statia, this shoe-shaped land mass is the upper portion of a dormant volcano that rises steeply some three thousand feet from the cobalt sea and descends sharply two thousand feet to the ocean floor. It was first discovered by Columbus in 1493 and was ruled by the Spaniards for one hundred and fifty years before it became the object of a tug-of-war among the British, French, and Dutch in the 17th century. It was finally claimed by The Netherlands in 1816.

To tour the island, seven or eight of us hire a van, complete with Belulah, a self-assured, amply-rounded driver-guide obviously of African ancestry, garbed in vivid magenta, vermillion and chartreuse floral-printed cotton. She conveys that the population, then under a thousand, was a mix of British, Dutch, Scottish, Irish, and African. Most could trace their last names back to half a dozen families. All of the pale-skinned, blonde, blue-eyed individuals, who appear to be plentiful if not predominant, are apparently related and somewhat inbred. The fate of Arawak and Carib Indians, who had at one time inhabited the island, is unknown. Belulah clearly knows her stuff.

As we snake along winding coastline roads and pass through a smattering of tiny white-washed, red-roofed villages, Belulah continues to articulate historical geographical, economic, meteorological facts. She elaborates upon mainstay industries, lobster fishing, rum production and lace making. She embellishes pirate folklore and points out suspected hideouts. And, as Belulah extols the virtues of the tropical rainforest, I distinctly and clearly recall her assurance, "Definitely not. There have never been snakes on this island and there are none now. Do not worry. No one has ever seen a snake on Saba."

The question about snakes came from me. In spite of my bravado in most situations, I am terrified of snakes. I am petrified of snakes. I am deathly afraid of snakes. Harmful snakes. Harmless snakes. Big snakes. Little snakes. Red snakes. Green snakes. Yellow and black snakes. Striped snakes. Any snakes.

My idea of torture is to be chased with a snake. My brothers chased me with a frog (and frogs I like), relentlessly pursued me in spite of my blood-curdling screams, to my haven behind a locked outhouse door. Thankfully, my brothers never knew of my snake phobia. No one, including my husband or maybe especially my husband, no one knew an easy murder would have been to throw me in a snake pit or lock me in a small space with a few snakes, none of them deadly. I had been selected as one of ten-most-afraid of snakes, from a thousand plus first year psychology students, for a systematic desensitization experiment. It hadn't worked.

****

As a Canadian prairie Grade 5 teacher, I opened my desk drawer one morning to discover a healthy-looking, harmless garter snake coiled atop the attendance register. Hushed students squirmed in their seats, eyes twinkling, corners of their mouths twitching, attempting to hide all-too-eager smiles. Others hunched with downcast eyes, hands covering grins that could not be suppressed. Whether or not there would be a snake in my desk drawer every day for the remainder of the season depended entirely upon my reaction.

It was one of those moments when, in emergencies, adrenalin takes over and transforms one into something one is not, one of those moments where one finds extraordinary presence of mind, or musters superhuman strength needed to hoist cars off of victims. Stuff like that. In one such moment, I managed to escape a vehicle submerged in water. In another, I somewhat miraculously freed my fingers from the closing automatic garage door. However, hell, this was one of my finest moments.

With my heartbeat thumping in my ears, like primitive drums around a bonfire, I smiled sweetly. After all, a sweet smile isn't so different from a sickly smile. I smiled sweetly and, in a voice that may have been half an octave higher than usual but not sufficiently squeaky to tip off the kids, articulated, "A snake. And what a lovely snake he is. Now, would someone please return him to his home?"

After one of the boys collected Snake, I proceeded with the roll call, my hands carefully positioned so that their tremble would remain unnoticeable... and to avoid touching the spot Snake had inhabited. Later, unseen, with paper towels, I scoured and scrubbed away any trace of Snake, although I could see none, wiped away any vestige that might have remained on the register cover or in my desk drawer.

****

This day, however, as we trek up Mount Scenery to the National Park and tropical rainforest beyond, my confidence has been boosted. After all, Belulah unequivocally declared 'absolutely no snakes'.

Palms, ferns, begonias, philodendrons, orchids, yes. Mahogany groves, if we reached the cloud-nurtured summit, yes. Parrots and a red-billed tropic bird, or two, if we were lucky. Monkeys, perhaps yes. Snakes, no.

First in line, I am bouncing, practically dancing up the approximate five-foot-wide dirt trail, spirit singing, soaking up glorious midmorning sun, attuned to tropical bird squawks from overhead trees. For some unknown reason, I glance downward. Perhaps it is a habit formed from scouring Statia's beaches for blue trading beads. Perhaps a premonition. Whatever. I stop dead. There, four inches in front of my bare sandaled toes, slithers a snake! A gigantic snake. A gargantuan snake. A dark-brownish-black snake, seemingly void of markings (although I do not claim meticulous examination), at least six (well, possibly five) inches in diameter, is sliding across the path, head hidden in underbrush to the left of the path, tail invisible on the right.

I have struggled in vain, during ensuing years, to recall what happened next. I cannot. The scene can only be reconstructed through the voice of fellow tourists.

"You came flying, I mean flying down the mountain, white as chalk, wild-eyed, hair streaming behind."

"What's wrong? queried Belulah, what's the matter? What happened?"

"Th... th... there's a huge snake up there."

"We have NO snakes on this island, she replied."

"I know a &*%$#@*& snake when I see one."

That was the first time I ever used the "f" word in public (unfortunately it wasn't the last). At least that's what I was told. I have no reason to doubt the truth of that statement. My insistence apparently propelled the 'guys' upward, to check it out. They later reported observing at least thirty feet of winding snake, seeing neither the head nor tail. I felt totally vindicated.

I otherwise recollect very little about the incident, or the day for that matter. Did others continue their trek into the rainforest? I don't know. I did not. Did an hour or more pass before we descended? I don't know. Suspended in time and space, I remained perched on a log, motionless, basking in the sun's comfort, like a snake would, I suppose, during the course of whatever it was that ensued. But I do recall the huge and rather sedating rum punch served in the restaurant bar before lunch.

Sporadic attempts, through the years and from the safety of my home, to identify Snake by searching encyclopedia and internet sources have been futile. Although anaconda seems the most logical choice, its resemblance is somewhat dissimilar. Perhaps it was a snake endemic to Saba, in the same way that species vary by island in the Galapagos.

So I never learned who Snake really was. I just know that he was comfortable in his environment. He was part of that Saba rainforest and probably had been for centuries. Islanders, however, denied his existence, perhaps due to unawareness, perhaps for their own benefit or otherwise. And I reacted 'it's him or me.' Fear, my own fear deprived me of a rare opportunity to experience a tropical rainforest, to explore the world in which Snake lived.

I have since pondered the analogy between my reaction to Snake and the manner in which we humans respond to others from different cultures, the way in which we interface with indigenous peoples or immigrants from foreign lands. How often do we sidestep situations we are afraid to face? How often do we avoid places in which we feel uncomfortable? How often does fear prevent us from connecting with the unfamiliar, from entering a world we do not understand? How often do we needlessly turn away? I might have stepped over Snake and kept right on going into the adventure of a lifetime, don't you think?

Sheila Carnegie

'VIVA LA VIDA' IN COSTA RICA

"Friends show their love in times of trouble, not in happiness."

Euripides

It was after I left Old Toad Island. Dee said I needed a change of scenery. She was right. I was 'moping' and did need a diversion. Moping isn't for Esmerelda. Dee made the reservations and insisted on an 'all-inclusive'. I was up for that. I didn't have it in me to arrange anything. It was a major feat if I managed to get out of bed each day, and the thought of a spa-like holiday was inviting.

Well, first thing I learned, it wasn't a spa. It wasn't even healthy. I didn't realize this, however, until the morning after we arrived. There is a reason guests are scheduled to flock in during the night, when you are unable to assess the location of your room, and are unaware of being squashed in with neighbours like sardines in a tin. You are oblivious to undersized pools, agouti (similar to large guinea pigs) scurrying through bushes, or monkeys clamoring through trees, waiting to cart off cameras, watches, whatever is set down. Whether or not you are nearby.

At our first breakfast I reach the conclusion that I am not here to improve my health. No yogurt, berries, and granola for Esmerelda. Hot and cold cereals, beans and rice, hash browns, stuffed tomatoes, muffins, toast, pancakes, tortillas, custom-designed omelets, scrambled, fried and boiled eggs, fajitas, ham, sausages, fruits, custards, cheeses, several types of pastries, juices, jellies and jams. There is so much it is difficult to choose. Hell, I can have a different feast every morning. And there are mid-morning snacks, a buffet lunch at 1pm, mid-afternoon refreshments, happy hour with more munchies, and a buffet dinner early evening. This is bound to be a foodie's heaven. Or so I think, that is until I look around me. Almost everyone is vastly overweight. Were they like this when they arrived? How long have they been here? Will I look like this when I leave?

Dee doesn't bat an eye over breakfast. "Isn't this all-inclusive thing great?" she chirps. She points to the three plates in front of her. "One for carbs, one for protein, one for veggies."

"Hash-browns, carrot muffins and custard are hardly veggies," I remind her.

"Says who?" she counters. I give up, console myself with the fact that at least my breakfast fits on one plate.

After breakfast, Dee insists our rooms are changed to pool level. "I'll tell them you have a heart condition," she promises.

"Thank god. If we have to climb three flights of stairs several times a day, I'm sure I'll develop one", I laugh. Little did we know what lay ahead. Mind you, stairs could be an advantage as far as weight gain is concerned.

Unfortunately, poolside rooms are not yet vacant. So we have no access to our luggage, which is locked in storage. Then, even after rooms have been readied, unless we haul our own luggage, we wait for porters. I am okay with this, more or less, but Dee is not. She sputters and marches off.

While I am huddling in the shade, sweating like a hog, waiting for our reassigned, air-conditioned room to be opened, I glance toward the pool. Dee is sprawled out on a deck chair, soaking up the sun. I have no idea where or how the hell she changed to her bathing suit. Maybe she slept in it. Or bought a new one. At her elbow is some exotic drink, obviously with orange juice, grenadine, a maraschino cherry, and god knows what else. Dee certainly knows how to vacation!

The poolside afternoon was uneventful. Well, more or less.

"Aren't you going for a dip?" Dee queries.

"With a heart condition?" I joke.

"Maybe the wading pool?" she retorts.

"I have no towel. I don't have a ticket to get one."

"What did you do with it?" she sounds annoyed. "I gave it to you when we checked in."

"Well, if you did, I don't have it. I looked through everything."

Dee sighs. "Maybe I can get another at the front desk later, if you come with me. Right now, let's hit the bar."

"Okay," I'm already on my feet, leaping at the chance to get out of the heat. I am not a sun lizard, like she is. The bar is cool, less than bright. And a cold white wine sounds refreshing.

The bartender is a young stud, muscular, dark-skinned with a blue streak running through his black, curly hair. What a shame, I think. Dee is of a different opinion.

"Wow!" she exclaims, "what a hairdo!"

"Yeah, complements the fuchsia in yours!"

"Esmerelda, he is a handsome dude. Don't be such a stick-in-the-mud…" she shields her mouth with her hand.

"What can I get for you two beautiful ladies?" he croons. The words slide off his tongue. This guy has had lots of practice.

Dee smiles widely, "a rum and Coke, and my friend will have a white wine."

As though I am invisible, can't speak for myself.

"White wine?" he stops short of sneering. He knows what is good for him… he may have noticed my facial expression. "How about a guaro?" he suggests.

"What the hell is a guaro?" I ask, working up my own sneer.

"Guaro is the national drink of Costa Rica. It's a liquor distilled from sugar cane juice. An 'aguardiente'. I can mix it with…"

"Let's try one straight up," Dee chimes in, as though she is afraid of losing his favour. "We're in Costa Rica, we must do this right."

"Dee, *aguardiente* is *agua* and *ardiente*, 'burning water', we…" I am trying to warn her.

He has already poured two shots. I take a sip and almost choke. Hell, if you ask me, this was certainly not misnamed. I ask to see the bottle.

"It is part of our culture," Johnny adds. Dee has already asked his name. Johnny, right. Probably Johnny Doe. "Viva la vida," he raises a glass towards us.

Dee stays at the bar, chatting and laughing with Johnny, in between his other customers. I plop myself on a nearby bar stool, quietly sip my firewater. Sometime later, I set down my empty glass. Dee is well into her second.

"Another?" Johnny asks. "Two shots and you'll be sweet," he encourages.

"Two shots and I'll be dead." I bid my farewells, turn on my heel, and seek the comfort of a soft bed and a good book in an air-conditioned room.

Dee bumbles, or stumbles in some time later.

"Are you sleeping?" she asks. I don't respond. "Wasn't that fun?" I hear her getting ready for bed. "Hey, whatda you know, I just found your pool towel ticket in my pocket."

I resist growling. I wonder if leaving Old Toad has somehow depleted what was once my sense of adventure.

****

The following day, we book a mid-morning boat cruise across the bay to a snorkeling site and BBQ lunch on the beach. It is a gorgeous, sunny day with calm seas reflecting fluffy cotton floating across a brilliant blue sky, the kind of day where nothing can possibly go wrong. Or so I think.

Seven passengers are aboard, two younger couples, a guy travelling solo, and us. Well, it takes Dee all of two minutes to complete introductions. She attempts to engage in a bubbly conversation with everyone, though primarily the fellow, another John, more or less our age, and obviously a Spanish-speaker.

The boat anchors near the shoreline, shallow enough for us to wade ashore. There are a few dozen others already on the beach. Dee is exploring the site, hopping around like a sandpiper, checking out everything and everyone. Sometimes, I wish I could be as 'social' as she. She quickly adapts to any environment.

We 'stake out' our territory with beach towels, hats, cover-ups, sandals, sunglasses, and hit the water, cool and refreshing. After half an hour or so, I'm back on the beach, lounging in a shady spot, enjoying the day. Dee and several of the others are still in the water.

I hear Dee's shriek before I see her. Then she is pushing herself toward the beach, plowing through the water like a water skier in competition or a woman gone insane. Shark? There is no fin, no blood. Others in the water are paying attention, but don't seem frantic. She stumbles on the sand, reaches our towels, and sinks down.

"What happened? What the hell…"

"Something bit me. It stings and itches like crazy. Look!" She points to red welts rising on her arms and legs.

A couple of other women, who followed her off the beach, offer, "Jellyfish. We think she was stung by jellyfish. We saw a number of them out there."

"Damn right, I swam through a whole school of them," Dee spits out.

"Okay," I ask, "so how dangerous is this? What do we do?"

Bad question. As soon as Dee hears the word 'dangerous' the situation worsens. I swear.

"It can certainly be miserable. There will be burning, stinging," one woman says.

"Very painful," offers another. "Perhaps numbness. She should try to bathe it with saltwater, vinegar, or even urine. She might need medical attention when the boat returns. There can be complications."

Dee hears all of this. It is not reassuring. She is frantic, almost clawing at herself, writhing in the sand. The welts have increased.

"What can I do? Should I get some saltwater? Vinegar? Do you need a container? The bathroom is over there…"

She is almost incoherent. In agony. One woman offers to get saltwater, another goes to the 'kitchen' to find vinegar. "They likely have some for a salad or something…."

I go look for a container, a jar, or glass, or plastic bucket, anything she can use to collect urine, if this is her choice.

After some or all of the 'medical remedies' have been administered, there is nothing left to do but wait for a boat and have lunch. She has no fever, and is neither dizzy nor nauseous, all of which are good signs, I understand. After a burger and a couple of beers, she settles down, but waits anxiously to board the first boat 'off the island'. I share her anxiety.

We are boating back to the resort. 'John' moves himself to be close to her. She is not in the mood. She raises her eyebrows and helplessly turns to me. I wrack my brain, trying desperately to recall what might be a Spanish word for 'bugger off'. I don't succeed. However, we get back and whip her into the resort medical clinic. *Viva la vida...* another day in Costa Rica.

****

After a quiet morning, Dee can no longer sit still. However, she is still suffering from jellyfish stings, and wants to do something where she doesn't have to move. I suggest sleep. She declines.

"I got a coupon yesterday," she is almost breathless with enthusiasm, "for a reception with wine and cheese, and other goodies."

"What type of reception?"

"It's a new resort wanting to tell people about their facilities."

"Time share, time share," I chant.

"It can't be that bad," she cajoles, "they say a total of thirty minutes."

"Time share, time share, high pressure sales," I warn her.

"Do this for me," she coaxes, "I am not well today and need some distraction from the pain and itchiness of these horrible stings."

She's got me. Plus I need a break from her complaints and irritability.

"Okay. Thirty minutes. No more."

"Let's go, ten minutes..."

She spruces herself up, pulls on a shirt with bling, spikes her hair, freshens her lipstick, and looks great as she always does, next to me, her 'country cousin'. She bounces out the door. I drag my feet, trying not to show my reluctance. I consider feigning jellyfish bites, or spider bites, or some damn thing.

The room for the presentation is in a grand ballroom, thick carpets, chandeliers, comfy chairs. It is apparent we are not the first people to arrive; the platters of 'goodies', primarily crackers and cheese cubes, are partially empty. The wine is awful. The 'hustlers' at the front of the room are licking their lips in anticipation, rather like wolves contemplating a rabbit dinner.

We listen to the 'spiel', in several different versions. I am leaning back, arms crossed. Dee is leaning forward, sitting on the edge of her seat. All symptoms of her jellyfish stings seem to have disappeared. It doesn't take too long before eye contact of the presenters leave me and are directed toward her. It takes even less time for my headache to slowly develop and reach a crescendo. No need to feign anything.

"Let's go," I mouth words to her. Several times.

She ignores me. I get up to refill my glass, and get some snacks. They ignore me. I leave the room once for several minutes. They ignore me. After nearly an hour, I exit again and make a quick return, interrupt the salesmen.

"Hey, Dee... do you know the hotel down the beach has an even better opportunity, at a lower price, with pool, Jacuzzi, complimentary drinks at the bar?"

Dee is intrigued. Now, in fairness, I am not actually lying, just playing a hunch. I know that Dee is a gambler, and the risks are those she is willing to take. Play the odds. I need to play the game.

"Really?" she perks up.

"Yep, really," I say.

"No, just wait a moment, we can do better... we will have a final offer, just give us a few minutes to consult," the salesman stammers.

"We can come back tomorrow," Dee promises.

"No, please, just a few more moments," he pleads.

"Tomorrow," Dee firmly insists. "Tomorrow."

I know I, for one, will not be back tomorrow or any other day. My head is throbbing, but I know I have won this round. I say nothing. Nothing except, "*hasta luego*," as I practically drag her out.

"Are you up to a *guaro*?" I almost beg. "And to hanging out with Johnny?"

"Yep. Let's hit the bar," she grins. She's forgotten about my promise of a better time-share offer. Or maybe she just needed a way to get out of there.

I personally think I might be able to handle two shots tonight. And secretly I hope we will both sleep well.

Viva la vida, another day in Costa Rica.

****

The final blow occurs two days later. After having spent the previous few days relaxing Dee is antsy. At breakfast she squeals, "I know what we can do. Go on one of those tours advertised on the board."

"Which one?" I am hesitant, noncommittal.

"Let's go zip lining! Are you up for zip-lining?"

"Zip lining?" My mouth falls open.

"Yep. Zip lining, in a forest valley. It will be fun, like we're flying."

"Hell, no, there is no way I'm going zip-lining."

"Oh, come on. Don't be a stick in the mud."

"I'd rather be a stick in the mud, than dead in the mud."

"It's safe. In a national protected area, in fact."

"Dee, I am afraid of heights. I cannot go up past the third rung of a ladder. I cannot stand on a balcony unless it is recessed. I am not going zip lining. It might be safe for others, but I'd likely have a heart attack from fear."

"Well, they say one needs to face fear and overcome it."

"I really don't give a hoot what **'th-ey'** say. **'Th-ey'** can go zip lining. I am not going."

"Party pooper," she pouts, "well, I'm going."

"Go for it. I know my limits. I will find something else to do. Maybe I'll go for a walk in the cloud forest."

"Right. You have your head in the clouds half the time anyway," Dee mutters.

"Well, then, I'm used to it. I don't have fears to face. This is a vacation, not a sports challenge or reality television," I reply.

With this, she turns on her heel and marches away. I don't see her for several hours during which I meander across swinging bridges through, and high above, a magnificent cloud forest, viewing luxurious greenery, exotic blossoms and tropical birds.

Shortly before dusk, Dee stumbles into our room. Her face is flushed, eyes wide.

"Are you alright?"

"No, I'm dizzy and my heart is pounding."

"Too much zip lining?" I ask. Big mistake.

"No!" I hear some expletives under her breath. "Of course not! The zip lining went fine. I faced my fear and overcame it. Maybe too much sun…" she trails off.

"You had a hat?"

She nods. "But the sun was hot."

"The doctor's office is a few doors down. I think you should get checked out… it could be too much sun, or maybe after-effects from the jellyfish. I'll come with you."

"Okay… okay," she agrees. She holds a cool, wet facecloth on her face and wrists. "Let's go."

The doctor asks about her recent activities, checks her blood pressure, listens to her heart, and orders an ambulance to take her to the nearest hospital. Just for observation he says. Dee declines my offer to ride with her.

A few hours later, there is a knock at my door. The doctor reports, "I'm quite certain she will be fine, but she needs rest. Her blood pressure is high, as though she experienced some sort of trauma, so we will watch her, and do some tests tomorrow." He smiles, neither of us mentions zip lining. So much for overcoming fear.

After two nights in the hospital (two days of R and R for me), on our last full day at the resort, Dee returns with a clean bill of health. However, subdued. Her spirit has been wounded, if not broken. I give her a huge hug, and we spend a quiet day. She lounges poolside in the sun; I read a book in the shade.

After breakfast in the morning, over mimosas at the bar, we bid farewell to Johnny Doe. No *guaro*, thank you very much. As we leave, we overhear one guy promise to have a liver cleanse when he gets home, while his companion contemplates checking into a detox center. The bane of all-inclusive resorts, I quietly think. I don't dare offer my opinion to Dee, who has previously sung their glories.

At checkout, we are handed coupons to enter a draw for a return trip. Providing we sit through a 'time-share promotion'. We glance at each other, simultaneously shake our heads, pocket the coupons, exchange 'high fives'. It is not because the resort has failed us. Nor because our friendship has faltered. It is karma. Salud! Viva la Vida!

Sheila Carnegie

RAMBLINGS FROM PORTUGAL

"And forget not that the earth delights to feel your bare feet and the winds long to play with your hair".

Kahlil Gibran

Hell, I knew that first night in Oporto, during the orientation session, this trip to Portugal was going to be trouble. One look at the tour guide was all it took. 'Stick Insect', as we subsequently dubbed her, is a short, skinny, barely-more-than-teenager, whose hair is striped like a badger and spiked as though she has stuck a finger in an electrical socket. Believe me, mine is nothing in comparison! She sports rings in her ears, nose, lip and various other body parts, some to which I cannot personally attest. Her greatest accomplishment, her greatest joy in life has been hiking the Alps. Several times.

If that isn't enough, the majority of the dozen or so tour participants, mostly 'Brits' and 'Aussies', introduce themselves with a gleeful recitation of countries they have visited and the kilometers accrued in each. Most of them wear pedometers, which Stick Insect insists we must have. Hell, I've never even seen one. This group has not come to 'ramble' through northern Portugal as the tour name promised; they have come to trek. To trek competitively, it seems.

This trip had been advertised as an 'easy-going exploration, requiring a low level of fitness and no special preparation.' Before signing up, I meticulously reviewed every detail, confirmed minimally required standards with the tour agent. Ever since that 'code-blue cardiac episode' I'll be damned if I take any chances. I'm not quite ready to bite the dust yet. Seemed, however, from the description, if one had the ability to cross a room on foot, or stumble around the block without crutches, one could easily handle this journey. Right.

The second day the true nature of the trip is revealed. We will apparently take a 'short day-jaunt' from the ancient pilgrimage town of Lamego to Peso de Regua, the 18th century village where we are staying for the night. Sounds pleasant, right? Until one discovers the distance is fourteen kilometers... fourteen kilometers through terraced vineyards of the port producing Duoro Valley. Give me a break! I mean who walks fourteen kilometers on a daily basis as a matter of course? Up and down and over steep-sided hills? Without special preparation? Even in a reasonably active life?

My options are limited. I can make my own way to Regua. Or I can die in the Duoro Valley. Not having sufficiently prepared for the latter, I choose the first, risking disdain from fellow travellers. On the back of a napkin, before she dashes off with the group (she never strolls, always dashes like a mad woman in urgent need of a washroom), Stick Insect scribbles directions to the bus station. I follow them. No bus station. I retrace my steps, start again. Still no bus station. I bite back panic. I am alone and more or less lost in a foreign country where everyone speaks a foreign language. However, I am not without resources.

I retrace my steps, return to the square where vendors sell their wares. I speak no Portuguese. They speak no English. But smiling, enthusiastic chatter, questioning eyebrows are universal. As are other forms of communication. I draw a picture of a bus, state my destination both verbally and in writing. Aha! Heads bob up and down. They grin. More chatter. Someone draws a map. Someone points, using fingers to count number of blocks and indicate left and right turns. I follow directions. Eureka! Bus station. Nowhere near the vicinity indicated by Stick Insect. It's surprising she made it out of the Alps.

The afternoon is a fine one. An interesting bus ride with locals through the picturesque valley. Conversation with English-speaking high school truants. Time to visit a 10th century cathedral, to observe cobblers at work, to meander through a market, to explore the streets and shops of Regua, to photograph Portuguese lifestyles. Opportunity to raise a ruby goblet of the Duoro Valley's finest, and witness the scarlet sun slip below the horizon.

Shortly thereafter the trekkers return, perspiring and panting. My roommate Roslyn, a vivacious, congenial, auburn, freckled, chunky Australian woman, flushed crimson, drenched in sweat, drags herself in, limping, flops on the bed, gasping, sucking as much oxygen into her lungs as she can. I pray she won't die.

That day, I am reminded that frequently, when things don't go according to one's plan, it is because something so much better has already been planned. Frequently, when one is denied, it is because a greater gift will be granted. My afternoon was obviously more enjoyable than hers. Later that evening, as we exchange stories, I tell her of my decision.

"I am going to continue to travel with the group, share meals, join the others when I can. But I will neither jeopardize my health nor suffer needlessly. I will not 'push the flow of the river'." The flow of my own river, that is.

The following day, I take a taxi to the summit in Montesinho Natural Park, where I peacefully await the others. For over an hour, I have seen no vehicles, no sign of human life, heard only whipping wind and melodious birdsong. This is one of the most desolate, most peaceful places I have ever been, a perfect opportunity to steel my senses for the onslaught of the trekking crew.

In time, two figures appear over a distant ridge. 'Boorish Bob', a swarthy, greasy-haired, short, stocky, gnome-like round-bellied creature, desperate to impress Stick Insect, leads the pack at her side, although he is trying to cover a distinctive limp. Others soon follow, in pairs or single file, multi-coloured pinheads dotting the hollowed plateau between us. My heart sinks like a stone in the ocean. The reverie is broken.

Stick Insect and Boorish Bob are first to reach me. She is bubbling and bouncing, he, sweating profusely, is puffing, gasping and wheezing. After the others arrive and resume normal breathing, together we begin our descent into a verdant valley, originally settled by Visigoth Germanic tribes. We make our way through windswept meadow toward oak and alder, ash and willow, chestnut and cork trees that have recently unfolded spring green. A metallic ribbon snakes through the emerald basin below. Wolves and deer, wild boars and wildcats, badger and otters apparently inhabit this area. We see none. Roslyn and I bring up the rear, stopping to admire and photograph wildflowers and some of the 150 species of birds that live here. Including a rare black stork.

The others stride forward, eyes fixed on the path before them, periodically call out over their shoulders, urge us to hurry along. Boorish Bob shouts, "Come on gals, get a wiggle on! Keep up with the group, will you?"

Roslyn and I simultaneously raise our eyebrows and grit our teeth. "He has already become Stick Insect's mouthpiece?" I ask.

She nods. But we do not change our pace. If anything, it slows. Roslyn mutters, "You were smart to take the taxi up. After this I'm with you. Short walks only. I've had enough self-punishment."

At Guadramil, and Rio de Onor on the Spanish border, we have stepped back in time. Both villages are communal, self-sufficient. Thick-walled stone houses appear as extensions of the landscape, appendages of cobblestone streets, reaching skyward. Their inhabitants, who approximate twenty in the first village and sixty in the second, are all older; young families have moved away for purposes of education and employment. It is apparent these people live in harmony with their surroundings in spite of the geographic and climatic limitations. Simplicity. Solitude. Serenity. Harshness.

That they follow a traditional lifestyle is equally as apparent. Water is dammed and directed to the village; a grist mill is driven by a waterwheel. Fields are being hand plowed, cultivated, seeded. Meticulous rows of tiny plants sprout from a huge vegetable garden. Pork sausage coils hang in the smoke house. A stuffed wild boar's head adorns a wall. I note its strange similarity to Boorish Bob.

With the exception of a few photographs and mutterings, few of our 'crew' seem particularly interested or appreciative. They rush through the streets, past an ancient winepress, still in use, communal laundry tubs and scrub boards, dovecotes, and beehives. They are so anxious to return to the trekking trail, they see nothing. I shake my head, shrug my shoulders. Hell, I cannot believe my fellow travellers. Roslyn and I poke through everything. What people in this community have retained from the past is absolutely amazing. Exactly what many of us are attempting to regain early in the 21st century with 'grow food locally' movements and 'hundred mile diets'. Perhaps, today, we have stepped back in time to the future.

Although I realize the seeds for separation from the group have already been sown, I have no idea they will sprout, flourish, come to fruition the very next day. About ten miles out of Chaves, we stop at the Pedra Bolideira, a huge rock split in two, balanced so that the massive larger section can be rocked by the touch of a finger. A fascinating landmark, classified as a national monument in fact. For a moment, just very briefly, mind you, I wonder what would happen if I push it with my entire hand. In the direction of Stick Insect and Boorish Bob. In retrospect, not so doing would become one of the top ten on my list... *Regrets in my Life.*

However, on this day, I am even more intrigued by the Outeiro Machado Boulder, a prehistoric sacrificial 165-foot chunk of granite, inscribed with mysterious hieroglyphics, possibly Celtic in origin. We are scheduled to stop there after lunch but, having already bypassed the oldest church in Portugal, a 12th century monastery, a 17th century museum and a tile factory, all of which were on the itinerary, I am cautious.

"Will we be stopping at Outeiro?" I query Stick Insect.

"Definitely. After lunch in Chaves," she replies.

"I really, really want to see it. Roslyn also." Roslyn's head bobs up and down like a marionette's. "If we're not stopping, we'll take a taxi during lunch hour. It's only two kilometers from Chaves, and we don't mind. We'd be back in time for the bus."

"No need to do so. We'll break for lunch in Chaves, then stop on our way out."

"You are certain? Promise?"

"Most definitely. I promise." She grins, raises one palm, as though swearing a statement in a courtroom.

You would think, having lived this long, having prided myself on what I had learned about the human condition, this would have been a signal. You would think I would have known better. However, we are both reassured. Stick Insect is convincing.

While the others trek to the pub, Roslyn and I scurry through the town. We marvel at the a sixteen-arch Roman bridge (78 AD), gobble sumptuous calzone-like pastries, layered with meats and cheeses and veggies, scamper to the thermal springs, admire a 14th century keep, a restored 11th century Romanesque church with a splendid pipe organ, and a magnificent 17th century Baroque cathedral, clad from floor to ceiling in 18th century *azulejo* blue tiles depicting New Testament scenes. We return to the bus at the pre-designated departure time. We wait. And wait. And wait.

An hour later they appear, tittering, joking, guffawing, a few with unsteady gait, some with slurred speech, a few silent in acquiescence. Stick Insect and Boorish Bob are last to board the bus, gazing into each other's dilated pupils, whispering behind their hands, giggling like schoolgirls. He has his hand on her back, or maybe her bum. I can't be sure. No explanation. No apology. No contrition.

Except for initial greetings, Roslyn and I maintain stony silence as the bus progresses on its way. Though I may have entertained a thought or two of revenge. That is until we pass the crossroad that leads to Outeiro Machado Boulder.

"Wait," I shriek, "just a minute. Are we not going to Outeiro?"

"Like the itinerary states. You promised!" adds Roslyn.

"Afraid not," Stick Insect calls out. "The pub took longer than planned. If we stop now we'll arrive at Geres too late to get in a walk before dark."

"And the rest of us want to do that," pipes up Boorish Bob. "You weren't there so we decided without you."

I cannot recall what I said next. If anything. Perhaps that is best. Whatever it was, I suspect it was under my breath or Roslyn would have cheered. But I do clearly remember and confess that at that moment my thoughts of revenge turned to those of violence, very briefly, of course. I lost any remaining shred of respect for Stick Insect. As for Boorish Bob, I had no initial respect to lose. And I do remember tasting port that evening. Several kinds. Several glasses. And I recall having an extra-long massage in the spa. I have no idea which event came first.

Somehow, that day was for Roslyn and I what the constitutional insurrections were to the 1820 rebellion in Portugal. The next day in Geres National Park, as the others whisk on by, we proceed at our own pace, or, if I am to be totally honest, perhaps saunter slightly more slowly than our usual pace. We examine Roman aqueducts from 78 AD and inscribed stone tablets marking the Roman Road, at one time the main military highway between Braga and Astorga in Spain. This is awesome! Here are the names of renown rulers including Hadrian, 121-134 AD, Antoninus Pius, 138-161 AD, Marcus Aurelius Antoninus, 161-180 AD, Gaius, 161 AD. Here endures history! It is easy to visualize brawny Roman warriors straddling magnificent, handsome steeds, riding in single file, caramel-skinned soldiers garbed in plumed and crested helmets, ornamented silver breastplates, red and ivory tunics above bare muscular legs... until Roslyn's voice returns me to reality.

We identify and photograph wild columbine, Solomon's seal, the rare Geres fern, heather, lavender, cedar, and white brome. We absorb freshly scented cool air, drizzling rain on our cheeks, a gurgling brook at our feet. And all the while we ignore Boorish Bob's insults, Stick Insect's chiding, and the call from others "to get on with it." Enough is enough. Of course, we are not being deliberately obstinate. However, we have come to ramble through northern Portugal and that we are determined to do. That, to us, is 'getting on with it'.

During the days that follow, when our fellow travellers trek, Roslyn and I create our own 'ramblings through Portugal.' They hasten through a country they never really perceive nor experience. We watch wool and linen-making demonstrations, scrutinize an oppressive 14th century castle tower which at one time caged a queen, smell the dankness of dungeons that imprisoned commoners, sense fear in catacombs, confront death in ossuaries, graveyards and glassed-door family crypts harbouring treasures of the deceased. Each cathedral has a spirit, energy of its own, and we almost always independently but identically identify its nature.

You wouldn't believe what two curious minds can discover and absorb. Necks of market place chickens are defeathered in a manner that denotes their geographic origin. Charcoal diagrams, rabbit tail erasers and 1000 Fahrenheit temperatures were used in the manufacture of blue tiles in azulejo panels, which reveal tales of past times. Apparent at a hilltop archaeological dig, Citania de Briteiros, an Iron Age settlement, dating back to the first century BC, inhabited by Celtiberias from 4th century BC to 4th century AD, are the 'bones' of family unit structures, communal baths and circular buildings, moats and drainage systems.

Hell, one morning we were port tasting at 9 am. Accidently, of course. We just jumped on a city tour bus that happened to stop at a port winery. Before breakfast. The real treasure, however, revealed itself after the tour was over, though I must admit the remainder of the tour is pretty much a blur.

We are wandering the streets, searching for Aguardente de Medronos, a fruit brandy made from Arbutus trees. I am particularly interested because there are many

Arbutus trees growing on Old Toad Island. Since my efforts at growing agave have met with little success, I'm seeking other alternatives for natural resource development, still trying to gain acceptance and respect from local gardeners and growers.

We happen upon a small shop nearby a huge church, antique, obviously significant, and wander in. "Roslyn, come here," I beckon, almost breathlessly, "look at these!"

She scurries to my side, "So what have you found now?" She knows my penchant for a treasure hunt.

I point to several baskets of body parts. For once, I am speechless.

Well, let me clarify… not real body parts, but body parts formed of a plaster-like substance. Roslyn and I glance at each other, eyebrows raised, pick up and replace, one at a time, a finger, nose, hand, foot, stomach, knee, liver, breast, penis, testicles, all humanlike.

"What are you thinking?" Roslyn grins.

"That we should buy Boorish Bob a gift?" I chuckle.

After some hesitation and attempt to communicate with a shop clerk, a woman emerges from a back room. It seems that if we have any illness or defect of any body part, all we must do is purchase the part, take it to the nearby church altar, and pray for healing.

Frankly speaking, I cannot imagine placing a breast on the altar to request enhancement or reduction or even tumour removal. And I sure as hell cannot imagine a man placing a plaster penis before the congregation to declare to the entire neighbourhood his impotence or venereal disease. Roslyn and I have several conversations about this experience. Maybe it was pre-historic, or connected with ancient tradition when the Church became established. Maybe it was a creative endeavor of some artist who needed money. Maybe it was a ruse for tourists. Regardless, to this very day, I have a big toe that sits on my bedside night table, just to remind me we are all vulnerable, and that drinking too much red wine can cause gout.

Initially the group seems relieved to be rid of us. We no longer impede their progress, hold them back from their daily crusades. Boorish Bob is preoccupied with the seduction of Stick Insect. Aussie Arnold, a six and a half-foot red-complexioned, hardy, outdoors, outback-type is preoccupied in trying to bed any one of the other females who will have him. The females, varied in age and amenities, with the exception of Stick Insect, are preoccupied in avoiding both of them.

I cannot say we really miss them either. And, though each night we rejoin them for the evening meal, I cannot imagine why. An attempt to be social? A good will gesture? Predictability? Or simply because it was included in the tour price? Always, the first half hour of dinner conversation is devoted to a competitive and statistical analysis of who clocked the most distance in the least time, the accuracy of these recordings, and the highest accumulated score. Can you believe this? And always, Roslyn and I are silent, observant, trying our damnedest to maintain decorum, civility.

Then the discussion turns to us. We are lectured on the 'colonization of Australia and Canada', the inferiority of 'young' countries and their 'plebian' citizens, the bastardization of the English language and the sloppiness of our speech, the lack of literature and fine art, and "awl of thawt, you know." And on and on. Don't get me wrong. Not everyone does this. Primarily Boorish Bob and a few followers. However, those who do not participate in insult and patronization are, to my way of thinking, culpable by complacency.

Inwardly sighing, gritting my teeth, bearing the tension in my shoulders and the tightness in my chest, night after night, I withstand this, put up with this crap, attempt to think of a placating response, in the name of... in the name of what exactly? Amiability? Civility? Masochism? Martyrdom? Each night, before we retire, Roslyn and I speculate in the dark, for hours, about writing a novel. It is always a murder mystery, always set in a hotel or a guesthouse or a convent, wherever we happen to be staying at the time. It is easier to identify the victims than it is to admit to identifying with the killers.

For days I bite my tongue. As does Roslyn. But me, Esmerelda? I ought to show more gumption than this. I am definitely not living up to my own expectations. That is, until the night Boorish Bob belittles Canadian wines. It is not uncommon knowledge that I have, for many seasons, been a modest wine drinker, that is, if I am to speak modestly. There are those who might question 'modest' but would not question my wine-tasting 'experience'. There are also those who might question my abilities as a sommelier. But they would not question that I partake in what pleases my palate. Or in whatever happens to be decent and available at the time. Whatever... Boorish Bob does not know this. And I am not about to let this, the granddaddy of insults, pass unnoticed. Hell, I mean this is hitting below the belt.

"And of which Canadian vineyards do you speak?" I smile demurely.

"Well... well, I cannot think of any names at the moment... hmmm, let me think..."

"And of which vintages do you speak?"

"Vintages?"

"Yes, vintages. And the labels?"

"Well... well... I remember *Baby Duck* and *Wild Turkey.*"

"Bob (I have a difficult time refraining from calling him 'Boorish Bob'), Bob, you are obviously behind times. When did you last visit the 'colony'?"

"Well... well... it was in the late sixties or early seventies, I guess."

I guffaw. Deliberately. Feign choking, in fact. "Really, Bob, you should update yourself. Canada has produced several award-winning wines in the last number of years (which I know is true. Thankfully he asks me for neither vineyards nor vintages). "We are right up there with fine vineyards all over the world. As is Australia. By the way, what notable wines have ever been produced by Great Britain?"

Boorish Bob, for the first time, wilts. He shrivels. He is wordless. Thwarted. Stymied. Though my memory momentarily flits to a small, scrawny girl, a year younger than her classmates but fast on her feet, flying after the school bully a head taller than she. He is so surprised he stumbles, trips and without hesitation, and as he lays momentarily defenseless in the dirt, she throws herself across him, flails harmless fists upon his body. His embarrassment ends his harassment of others, especially girls. So it would be with Bob. Sometimes it just takes courage to rid oneself of a nemesis.

Roslyn grins, gives me a thumbs up. Stick Insect frowns, fingers the ring in her lip as though she doesn't quite comprehend what has occurred, offers no consolation to Bob, a deflated shell of his former self. He could now use the gifts we resisted buying him. It seems he is not the man about town she had been led to believe. It seems their ardor has been dampened. The others, after a respectful silence, quietly resume conversation. Someone, for the first time, asks about our discoveries that afternoon.

Gradually, in ensuing days, several of our fellow travellers become increasingly enthused to hear our adventures. Some of them privately confide that they would really prefer to join us but lack the courage to 'walk away', no pun intended. So sad, I think.

When they ask, we tell them. Hell, do we tell them! About the sights and smells and sounds and wisdom of the streets. Where to sample port at nine in the morning. Free. Where to shop for plaster body parts used for religious sacrificial 'healing' purposes. Where to buy the best pastries, *valdo* (a wine) and *medronheira*, a liqueur made from arbutus bark. Culinary specialties we have tasted, cuttlefish, octopus, pigs' ears, sea bass, *aguadente* (local "firewater"). Various versions of *bacalhau*, a national dish. Who the great Fado singers are and where to purchase CD's. Where to find a doggy barbershop, street theatre, or stilt entertainers.

And we tell them about the 'coup de grâce'. In fact, we can barely restrain ourselves. We lunch in a small, out-of-the-way outdoor café, where we order tripe. The balding, dark-eyed, white aproned, moustached, round-bellied owner, cook and waiter, cannot believe his ears.

"Tripas?" he asks. Three times. "Tripas? Sím? Tripas???"

Each time we nod. I mean how can you visit Portugal and not try tripe? He gets a menu. Points to the tripe. We nod. He brings us a photo. We nod. Like little kids offered a double-decker ice cream cone (though we are not as certain it will taste quite the same). Finally convinced, he too nods, breaks out in a smile that could span the Strait of Gibraltar, raises a finger as if to say *un momento*, turns and disappears into the kitchen. In a flash, he returns with crusty bread and olives for us to enjoy while he prepares the tripe. We wallow in warm sunshine like basking Mexican iguanas, grateful for the day.

He eventually returns with the *Tripas Oporto*, served with white beans in a tomato sauce. He stands by, holds his breath. "Yes! Absolutely delicious!" we grin, thumbs up. And it was. He bounces up and down, nodding, beaming, gesticulating. He calls out to a tall, silver-haired, slightly bent, stubble-bearded, beaming passerby who comes off the street, watches us demolish the *tripas*, vigorously claps his hands together high above his head, in glee, in admiration, dancing a step or two to non-existent music. Non-existent to our ears, that is. Three or four others have joined in cheering us on. By the time we empty our plates, the small crowd that has gathered breaks into applause. Several bow in a gesture of respect and esteem.

After considerable questioning in our less than fluent Portuguese and their less than fluent English, we are apprised of the *best tripe* competition between Lisbon and Oporto. Our appreciation of this national dish is the greatest honour and tribute we can pay them. *Rambling through Portugal* at our own pace has paid off. We've hit 'pay dirt'. Without pedometers. We have found 'the spirit of Portugal'. Rambling, that is.

Sheila Carnegie

ONE NEVER KNOWS

"The meeting of two personalities is like the contact of two chemical substances: if there is any reaction both are transformed."

Carl Jung

She floats onto the veranda of an old plantation house in St. Kitts, her feet barely brushing the worn wooden boards beneath. Others have already gathered for pre-dinner drinks, as is their custom. She arrives fashionably late, as I am to learn is her custom, pauses at the entrance, sweeps the room with one continuous motion. Only when assured her presence has been duly noted, she wafts in, drifts among guests like a helium balloon maneuvering through space, nods to those she has previously met, pauses for the proper introduction to others she has not.

She towers near six feet. Her bony frame, skinny as a cat's scratching post is garbed in swishing grey silk, the lace at her throat bejeweled with a gigantic cameo, a burgundy paisley pashmina shawl drawn tightly around her narrow, slightly hunched shoulders. I estimate her to be in her late sixties, although this assessment is belied by a crevassed face and grey hair drawn tightly into a bun at the nape of her neck. Her appearance and attire communicate affluence, lineage, aristocracy. Her manner, however, soon betrays her.

The paunchy, blue-eyed, silver-haired, genial Colonel, in pale lemon cotton slacks, black open-necked polo shirt and tan leather sandals, already sipping his second, or perhaps third gin and tonic, introduces her as 'Elizabeth Wellington'.

"Elizabeth Victoria Villiers-Wellington", she corrects in a raspy, crow-like voice as she proffers her hand, ringed with diamonds and emeralds too large to swallow. The spectacles perched on the tip of her hawk-like nose bobble when she speaks. That one should be graced by her very presence is apparent, to her if to no one else. The response she expects, however, is less clear. Is one to bow, curtsey, brush with one's lips the extended hand? Or shake it? What is appropriate in this otherwise casual setting? In the presence of a prima donna?

"I am a renowned author of classic English literature", she croaks in a thick British accent, "surely you have heard of my work?"

"No, madam, I am very sorry. I think not. I haven't studied English Literature," I lie, wondering why her name evades me. "What are some of the titles? Perhaps I'll recognize them."

"Ohhhh, I have been very successful. I'm told my work is right up there with that of Virginia Woolf and Daphne DuMaurier." She disdainfully tosses her head, flicks her ruby-adorned wrist, glides toward someone obviously more worthy of her presence.

I knowingly glance toward my mate. His raised eyebrows say all that needs to be said. From across the terrace, the colonel winks, flashes a corroborating grin in our direction. Later, he is careful to seat her and us at the opposite end of the dining room table. One would have to be in a separate building, however, to escape her superciliousness, her pomposity and narcissism.

Over a late night cognac in our room, a renovated cylindrical stone sugar mill, my partner and I, deciding to thereafter refer to Elizabeth as 'Lizzie' which is the same name which graced the famous Statian iguana, dismiss her as someone we prefer to associate with from a distance, from across the veranda, or preferably from another solar system. Arrogance and I have never become friends.

Life has since taught me that dismissing anyone on the basis of first impressions is premature if not unwise, perhaps an arrogance of a different sort. Even if our initial perceptions are accurate, there is no way of predicting the fallout of interactions... the impact of a benign statement, the interpretation of a situation over time, the connection spawned by an innocent, unknowing exchange.

****

My miniscule Affenpinscher, Brutus, had no idea that when he squared his jaw and jutted out his chin in determination, or when he leapt three feet into space to protect me from whom he believed was an attacker, he would inspire within me strength and courage, a resolve that would serve me well for years. My mother could not have known that some thirty years after her death her words would continue to echo through the room as clearly as they did in their first spoken moments. And for several decades I remained unaware that the twenty minutes I spent with a former student recovering from yet one more failed suicide attempt had influenced a turnaround and returned him to life.

As I was to learn, life is fraught with such examples. However, on this night Lizzie was shelved, deliberatively removed from conscious thought. Had we known the future role this woman would play, the good turn she would one day render, however, we may have very well determined otherwise.

****

119

The Colonel, a retired British Armed Forces officer, and his wife Margaret opened the inn after a newly elected government confiscated their sugar cane plantation, leaving them only the land and buildings immediately surrounding their home. They converted a portion of their house into lounging and dining areas, remodelled workers' cottages into suites, installed a swimming pool, edged the constricted property with blood-red poinsettia hedges. They planted magnificent herb, vegetable and flower gardens bordered by curving flagstone pathways and interspersed with walkways winding among hibiscus and roses, delphiniums, lilies, lavender and baby's breath, a panoply of ruby, emerald, sapphire, amethyst and ivory, gold and bubble gum pink. My 'black thumb' was envious.

The Colonel's affability, joviality, ease with guests, along with Margaret's kindness, helpfulness, quiet grace and organizational abilities, render them natural hosts. Their son, Philip, however, tall and stately, in fact rather like Prince Philip in terms of stature, appearance and formality, is not. He is stiff, proper, finds conversation difficult, and is redeemed only by Frances, his fiancée, whose ready smile and bubbly warmth is more notable than even her splendid freckled face and glorious auburn hair. Philip and Frances have journeyed from England to 'apprentice', to learn the business that will one day be theirs. At least that is the hope, the intent of Margaret and the Colonel.

Philip is assigned to transport Lizzie, along with other interested guests, to a neighbouring batik studio and shop, proffering hand-dyed fabric, handcrafted household furnishings and clothing. The first morning, after our half-hour wait alongside the vehicle, Lizzie wanders across the lawn, fashionably late as usual. Each morning thereafter, for a week, Philip, with the stoicism of a tin soldier, transports Lizzie on her quest for a uniquely designed fabric befitting her bloodlines. In spite of invitation, none of us had any inclination to join them.

Each day, a few hours later, they return empty-handed. Each evening, she announces to terrace guests that her search has been futile, that she has found nothing appropriate among those 'dreadful' textiles. She seems either oblivious to or disrespectful of the fact that several of us are now wearing those 'dreadful textiles'.

On the eve of her departure she declares that she has ordered, or rather purchased (since the batik artists, clever people that they are, demand payment in advance) her treasure. In accordance with her directions, several meters of fabric will be custom-dyed in her favourite garden hues, rather akin to Monet's paintings, or so she boasts, and then fashioned into a garment she has personally designed. She will collect it on her vacation the following year. We, and 'we' encompasses all guests except those that have arrived a few hours previous, we nod, smile politely, wish her well. A few women mutter regrets that they unfortunately will not see her '*pièce de résistance*'; others are obviously relieved to reach the end of what has become a fashion saga. Hell, to be honest, a torturous ordeal.

After Lizzie departs for her next destination, a private island that none of us can afford, or so we are informed, we learn of her background from other guests. Her wealth has not been accumulated by her writing success. In fact, no person of Lizzie's acquaintance is aware of her writing anything other than a shopping list. Her affluence and social position was attained by her marriage to a 94-year old aristocrat, an earl, or lord, or someone of similar stature. A nobleman, an old crock who on his deathbed, so to speak, wed his maid in exchange for her commitment to tend to his three Corgies, two terriers, six cats and a cockatiel, all of which mysteriously disappeared within the first year of his demise. There apparently existed considerable speculation among villagers as to whether the critters were disposed of or had simply escaped.

****

Our return to St. Kitts the following year is easy, joyful, rather like a reunion with old friends. At least that is the case with the Colonel, Margaret and Frances. Philip, however, remains remote. Although the warmth beneath his veneer is apparent, to break through his barrier of formality is daunting, a formidable task, one which we have not yet managed to achieve, in spite of several attempts.

When, on the third evening, Lizzie sweeps on to the terrace, our chins drop. We had deliberately arranged to be on the island when she was not. However, as karma would have it, at the last minute she changed her plans. In her words, "I simply cannot bear to spend the remainder of my vacation without the exclusive batik gown. My next stop, after all is the private island, and absolutely nothing else will suffice. I simply must have it."

The next morning, shortly after the crack of dawn and twenty minutes prior to the batik shop opening, Philip collects Lizzie, who proffers a royal-like wave from the rear auto window as they crawl up the driveway. They return a couple of hours later. Lizzie sashays from the vehicle, clutches a brown paper, string-wrapped parcel, presses it tightly to her breast as one might the Shroud of Turin. She says nothing but nods, smirks like a kid with a secret. Philip also nods, smiles ever so slightly, glances skyward. His sigh is barely audible, sounds more like air being slowly released from a punctured tire. His mission has been accomplished.

That evening, as the sun sinks below a golden, scarlet horizon, we gather on the terrace for pre-dinner drinks, as is our custom. That evening Lizzie is late, as is her custom. Excitement swells in anticipation of her entrance.   Several ruminate about her self-fashioned creation.   Suddenly in she swoops.   Swoops in like a condor, flapping outspread wings… a condor dipped in the dye vats of all of Calcutta's textile mills combined.   There she stands, covered from head to toe with scarlet and tangerine and lime and purple and lemon and fuchsia and gold and lilac and chartreuse and emerald and indigo and chocolate and bubble gum pink.   A cacophony… yes, a cacophony of colour.   Funny how a panoply of garden hues has metamorphosed into a cacophony.   Discord. Disharmony. Dissonance.   Monet must be rising from his grave at the very moment.

A moment of jarring silence is audible.   Then a single gasp, a collective intake of breath.   Followed by Philip who, facing me from a few feet away, blanches, mutters beneath his breath, "Oh my god!"

Our eyes lock.   My mouth twitches, threatens to smile.   He realizes I have heard him.   I nod in agreement. Give him a thumbs-up.   For some seconds, unnerved, he raises one hand to his brow, covers his eyes, bites his lip, remains frozen like Michelangelo's David.   Then the unexpected occurs.   He grins in my direction, returns the thumbs-up.   Thanks to Lizzie, the barrier between us has been razed.   Without her knowing.

Retreating once more behind his veneer, he gently clasps Lizzie's elbow.   "Shall we go to dinner?"

As he escorts her to the dining room, she rasps, "Oh, my dear, dear Philip, this gown is so-o-o gorgeous, so-o-o splendid. You must see how everyone adores it. Tomorrow I must return to the shop and select fabric for a second."

The Colonel winks in our direction.   So does Philip. Just after he suppresses a groan that slightly rumbles like a far-off tremor beneath Earth's surface.   Just before he grins, teases, "Would you care to join us?"

Sheila Carnegie

EXPLORING THE ARCTIC

"We need to save the Arctic not because of the polar bears, and not because it is the most beautiful place in the world, but because our very survival depends upon it."

Lewis Gordon Pugh

I am standing on top of a glacier, somewhere near Greenland. Who would have thought? Esmerelda on a glacier... of her own free will? Can you believe this? Hell, I can hardly believe it. I hate the cold. I must have had one glass of wine too many when I signed up for this one. Or maybe was rowing with one oar at that particular time, if you get my drift. At any rate, here I am, perched on the ice like a penguin in the Antarctic. You can be certain, however, I won't be diving into the waters any time soon. I am not that removed from reality.

Actually, once past the shock, I have to admit this is rather spectacular. Icebergs are floating in the bay beyond, with what appears to be a turquoise light shining from within. I peer around at icefields as far as I can see. It feels rather like 'I am king of the castle', or 'ruler of the world'. That is, until I free my fingers from my glove to photograph. When they begin to turn blue, about the same time as a huge chunk of ice calves with a huge crack that sounds beneath my feet, I decide to return to safer ground. That is, if one can find any.

At this time (2005), the glistening ice cap constitutes some 90% of Greenland's massive land surface. However, we are told that within the past year alone, ice fields have receded by 14%. As I write this (2016), the ice cap apparently constitutes approximately 80% of the country's surface. I fear for the future; I fear for muskoxen, polar bears, caribou and reindeer. I fear for hunters, all Inuit, for the North, and ultimately for the world.

****

Our plane from Ottawa landed on the runway at Kangerlussuaq airport, built by Americans in WWII. Greenland at this time of year is actually green, as was reported centuries ago by Erik the Red. The contrast between shimmering white ice and green is breathtaking. Glacier tongues snake down the fiords, spilling ice into the sea. We board the *MS Explorer* and set sail past multi-hued pre-Cambrian cliffs of Sondrestrom (Southern Stream fiord).

The second day, we reach Sisimuit, our first port of call, a small fishing harbour perched on rock. In thick fog, we anchor in the 'soup' (which I surmise is termed 'soup' due to various items afloat), and await our dockside berth, usurped by a huge cruise liner. Of all the nerve! Same old story... they are bigger than we are and carry more clout. Also, they likely pay higher docking fees.

We are not without entertainment, however, while we wait. We get an explanation of the welcoming ceremony, well, the one we would have had if we had gone ashore, or the one we might yet have. It is an Inuit custom, to light a qulliq (or kudlik) lamp, usually carved from soapstone, frequently crescent-shaped with wicks of arctic moss or cotton grass, or other natural materials from the tundra. Most frequently, they burn seal oil or blubber, though occasionally whale muktuk. What was once used for lighting, heating, cooking and drying clothing now primarily has ceremonial purposes. The 'keeping of the lamp' ceremony signifies lamplight to guide family members home, or welcome strangers travelling by. A lovely sentiment, but I sure as hell won't be making my home on a massive hunk of ice.

An emergency exit drill is coordinated by the safety officer, Vitaly. He declares, "You will broke your face if you jump in water and not put hand in life jacket." Best I not say more except that we get the message.

The highlight of the day, however, is a demonstration by a competitive kayaker, Number One in Greenland, to be accurate. He submerges himself in water only slightly above freezing, in roll after roll, always promptly righting himself, as one must in various weather and sea conditions. As a finale, he paddles off upside down in an inverted kayak, with only arms and paddle showing above the surface of the sea. I start shivering just watching. In fact, it becomes pretty clear to me why he is Number One. He is likely the only one competing in seas as icy as these.

The following days in Greenland resemble each other. We visit places with names I don't dare try to pronounce, but many of which I will remember. Illulissat, inhabited by the Dorset 2500-1000 years ago, in Qaasuitsup Municipality, is north of Arctic circle, and the home of many sled dogs. Sermermiut, named after 'people who live beside the ice' (don't they all?), is a 4000-year-old UNESCO archeological site with thirty Thule sod houses, occupied until early 20th century. Saqqaq, which name I'll remember for Scrabble (even though the game doesn't have enough q's), is a settlement that dates back to 4500-3000 years ago. Bones, or parts thereof, from middens can be seen sliding down bank edge to the sea. The guides tell us they are from sea mammals, not humans, but I admit I am skeptical. I mean until they are tested, how does anyone really know? I don't think it takes a brain scientist to figure out there are likely to be more humans buried on land than sea mammals.

In various places, we gingerly maneuver atop ice cliffs, visit museums, sod houses, old churches and archaeological excavations, view skin umiaks, ancient bones, Inuit art and carvings. We play musical games, and lose both a soccer tournament and a baseball game (which says a lot about people who take cruises, at least those to the Arctic). We pretend to enjoy an outdoor BBQ of seal, muskox, caribou, reindeer, capelin, along with salad and potato salad, for those of us who have lost an appetite for protein. I mean, who can really enjoy a hunk of what could be Santa's Rudolph? Thank god for coffee so strong it pretty much obliterates all other flavours.

Little do we know this was a mere appetizer for the raw meat smorgasbord yet to come, one that would leave blood dripping down one's chin. Not mine, mind you. I have been called many names and accused of many things, but being a vampire has never been one of them. At least not to my knowledge.

From Qeqertasuaq, the very large island, termed Disko Island by the Danish, recently calved icebergs are pushed out of Isfjiord into the bay. They will float across Davis Strait to Baffin Island and Labrador, and face their end off Newfoundland's coastal warm waters of the Gulf Stream.

At Uumanaq we are privy to a musical performance by a church choir, outfitted in traditional garb. Women wear embroidered and beaded garments and long sealskin kamiik (leggings), national masterpieces that take four women a year to complete and sell for five to six thousand US dollars. Men are attired in black trousers with a traditionally cut white cloth anorak.

We visit Qilakitsong (sky hangs low), an ancient burial site of Thule and Inuit, and the 'Greenland Mummies' overhanging the cliff edge, as wells as Agparsuit and Upervavik. At some point, I suspect because most of us have a terrible time pronouncing any of these names, let alone remembering them, we are given opportunity for an onboard lesson in the Inuktitut language. I last about five minutes. Or less. Which is more than I would have managed in the icy ocean, where a few brave souls (or 'idiots', depends how you look at it) decided to join a few (they aren't all stupid) of Greenland's swim team and take a dip. Hell, had they promised me a bottle of the best cognac in the world, I would not have joined them, although if the truth were told I might have entertained the thought. Briefly, that is.

Weather varies, though it is frequently foggy, particularly during morning. With wind and rough seas, the boat heaves, along with passengers. In Davis Strait, on our way to the Canadian side of the Arctic, for over an hour, the ship maneuvers through ice. Icebergs. Huge. I kid you not. They are battering the ship with more regularity than I hoped to hear, threatening to crunch all of us to bits. I think of the Titanic. In retrospect, I regret having seen that movie. I also recall the Inuit belief that time and space is a circular or spiral process as opposed to the Western concept of time as linear and unidirectional. 'A long time ago in the future' pretty much sums it up. I plant myself close to the exit where lifeboats are kept. No way am I going down... not again.

Once more there are more name places to remember, though these sound a little more familiar, and these I can pronounce. Feachem Bay in Buchan Gulf, Eclipse Sound, Cape Graham Moore, Bylot Island, all in the Baffin Region, Nunavut. At Cape Graham Moore we see bird cliffs, where hundreds of thick-billed murres and kittiwakes raise their young, at Salmon Creek a Thule site. Cold, majestic towering Baillarge Bay Cliffs, reflect gold and blue into cold seas and harbour white hare, arctic fox, peregrine falcon, ringed and bearded seals, eider duck and chicks.

Devon Island is the site of a former outpost, established in the late 1920's, early 30's, where two constables developed a strong dislike for each other. Their situation somewhat resembled War of the Roses. They painted a line down the middle of the cabin, and neither was permitted to invade the space of the other. Mysteriously, no one can quite explain what happened to either of them. I have a great time imagining the finale for this situation, especially having been previously and less than happily married. And we weren't imprisoned in a relatively small space through an Arctic winter, with deadly weapons.

At Pond Inlet, narwhals came into town. Big mistake. To be honest, I wish I had been elsewhere. Local hunters were frenzied. This was obviously a big deal. Guns and harpoons, buoys to keep bodies afloat, no holds barred, until the quota was met. Blood streamed into the sea. The entire village rushed to the beach, dancing and cheering, preparing for a celebration. I could not share it. The first narwhals I had ever seen, magnificent creatures relegated into huge inert hunks being chopped into muktuk, shared, and hauled off on four-wheelers. Perhaps I have never been sufficiently hungry to appreciate what this means to those who live here.

The Arctic tundra is often described as 'bleak', 'barren', obviously by those oblivious to its wealth of treasures, ice-sculptured shores, polar bears, walruses, a pod of some eighty belugas, spouting and churning water as they feed along the shore, a single bowhead whale, snorting and huffing. At this time of year, a prolifically blooming landscape unearths Arctic poppies, cotton grass, tiny delicate mushrooms, lichens, gorgeously coloured, miniscule flowers. Spiders, butterflies, hairy caterpillars are on the move, and depending on the location and distance of trekking, one can see bones galore, sod houses, tent rings, meat caches, whale skeletons, scat of both muskoxen and polar bears. Frankly, although scat is rather unexciting, I would rather meet their scat than the real thing.

At Port Leopold and Prince Leopold Island, off Somerset Island, Nunavut, we visited the PlJg-4 historic site associated to Parry's search of the Northwest Passage in 1819 and the James Clark Ross's search for the 1845-47 Franklin Expedition. We went ashore on Beechey Island, to the remnants of the site where the first three of Franklin's 128 men met their fate in 1945 overwintering on the island. Desolation is overwhelming in the summer; it is difficult to imagine what men faced in the winter; they must have had no idea of obstacles and tragedies ahead. From the gravesite, down the beach to Northumberland House, was situated the storehouse established by the Belcher search party in the event that Franklin survivors should return.

Thank heavens, a lighter side of this journey balances the somber side. Ashore, we are entertained by Inuit throat singers, musicians, games experts, dancers, and softball teams. On board, we enjoy fiddle classes, cocktails, a sing-song, cocktails, a musical talent show, cocktails, special theme dinners with Chardonnay, a Viking raid and, of course, more cocktails. One would think 'they' were attempting to disguise performance mediocrity with alcohol.

The highlight is perhaps the Scotch label design competition, though I have yet to determine the relevance of Scotch to an Arctic expedition. Perhaps it is a way of recycling obviously and previously emptied bottles of Scotch. The design winner, deemed so by a panel of judges, receives a bottle of Scotch, the only full bottle remaining aboard, I strongly suspect. After carefully scrutinizing the demeanour of the judges, I conclude they are responsible for emptying the Scotch to provide bottles for the contest.

Sheila Carnegie

In Resolute Bay on Cornwallis Island, as we wait out a rainstorm until our charter plane can come in the next day, I contemplate my experience in the Arctic. Hell, I do not belong here, that is for certain. It is too cold, too vast, harsh and desolate. But it has its rewards in addition to the miracle of wildlife... magnificent ice sculptures formed by nature, calving icebergs cracking, at times whipping wind, at other times silence but for the sound of gently lapping waves or bubbling streams, whispering breezes, wing beats of raven. Always a sense of agelessness. Providing we learn how to care for what we have.

AMAZONAS ADVENTURE

"We are the only species with the power to destroy the earth and also the capacity to protect it."

His Holiness the Dalai Lama

In a wooden boat, not unlike the freighter canoes used in parts of northern Canada for whale watching (formerly whale hunting), my fellow travellers and I, previously unacquainted, are motoring along the Cuyabeno River in the Amazon Basin. Dense, tropical rainforest towers on both sides of the partially shadowed river. In other words, we are in the jungle, in Sucumbios province, near the Colombian border.

The journey here was not uneventful. Several times, in fact, I questioned what the hell I was doing. When we crossed over one of the two highest passes in Ecuador, my teeth chattered with cold. Thankfully, they are still my own or they may have fallen out, especially while I was gasping for oxygen.

And wouldn't you know, as we approach Reventador Volcano, which stretches some 12,000 feet to the heavens, it spits up a huge plume of ash. Now, I don't know when this volcano last erupted, but it definitely is still active, and threatens to spew red-hot lava any second. Our guide stops the vehicle so we can photograph. I'm thinking he should be turning around and heading back in the direction from which we came. No one else seems particularly worried, but I keep my eye on that mountain until we are well past it. I try to close my mind to the fact that in a few days we will be returning, and Reventador will still be there. Waiting. I wonder if there are volcano gods and what an appropriate sacrifice might be.

I learned a lot on our journey to Cuyabeno Wildlife Reserve, in the Ecuadorian area referred to as the Oriente. I learned that Spectacle Bears do not hang out or cross roads where signs claim that they do. Perhaps their spectacles help them read signs and avoid those places they knew we would be watching.

I learned that in Napo province, near Baeza, in years past, Quijos men would fast for two months prior to the birth of their children, to ensure their safe arrival into the world. They ingested only water and marijuana juice, supposedly for medicinal purposes. Fifty percent of them died before their offspring were born. So why would they do this? Could marijuana have been an incentive?

Along the route, magnificent waterfalls are abundant. Cascada Magica on Rio Malo in El Chaco is truly magical. Cascada San Rafael, highest waterfall in Ecuador, borders the provinces of Napo and Sucumbios and is considered one of the country's natural wonders. To remember names for more than two would be stretching my limited memory bank, which recently prefers to treasure spectacular images more than words.

Lago Agrio, where we will stay overnight, is officially named Nueva Loja, and was formed in the sixties as Texaco's base camp. During a drought in Loja, many of its residents moved to this area to work in oilfields. Ecological degradation and obliteration of tropical rainforest characterizes the surrounding area. Miles of pipeline extend all the way to Quito. I bite my tongue. Good thing Sheila isn't here... she would have something to say without question. Then we'd both be in trouble. In fact, we could well be kicked off the tour.

Somewhere between Cascada San Rafael and Lago Agrio, the tour vehicle begins protesting. Intermittent beeps are sounding from the dash and, from where I am seated, I can see red alert messages popping on and off. The air conditioner stops. Power windows no longer work. The driver/tour guide and his assistant have become very quiet. I know we are in trouble. Hell, I don't want to be stranded on the highway, but I know better than to ask any questions. I don't want to create panic among the passengers. Besides, I haven't yet learned, thank my lucky stars, that there is a travel advisory, warning people to take precautions against robbery and violence in this zone. Had I known that, quite another scenario might well have unfolded. It is possible restraints may have been justified.

The vehicle limps into Lago Agrio, crawls across a lane of traffic and conveniently, with the driver's help, comes to a halt in front of a service station that advertises batteries, among other things. After the 'guys' locate the battery under the floor of the front seat, confirm its recent death, and the need for additional examination, we are taken by another vehicle to our hotel. Political parades crowd the streets, reroute traffic. Streets are fraught with activity and noise far into the night. Some hotels, or at least some rooms in hotels, have showers minus hot water. So you see, I am not exactly impressed with this city. It is, however, the gateway to Cuyabeno. The vehicle will be repaired, and we aren't stranded in the middle of nowhere. Gratitude leaves no room for complaint.

So here we are, the next day, motoring along the river in the Cuyabeno Wildlife Reserve, approximately 2300 square miles in size, the second largest of forty-five national parks and protected areas in Ecuador. Situated near the Colombia border, in the Amazon Basin, it spreads across approximately 1.5 million acres in Putamayo Canton, Sucumbios Province and Aquarico Canton in Orellana

Province. The area from the foothills to the jungle is rich in biodiversity and variety of species.

In no time at all, squirrel monkeys are spotted. The boat slows in black waters, cuts its engine so we can observe them, flitting among the trees, in their natural habitat. A mother carries a baby tightly clinging to her back. Before we leave a few days later, we will see several of the ten or twelve types of monkeys... spider monkeys, mustached tamarins, capuchins, howlers, and saki Monkeys, hooded with fur, to name a few. Actually, I think I've done well to remember these.

The next wildlife we see is less entertaining... at least personally speaking. A black-headed snake, somewhat camouflaged, slowly winds itself through tree branches overhanging the river. Now that wouldn't necessarily be a bad thing... another boatload of tourists is closer than we are, pointing and photographing. However, when they leave, our driver, and I don't know what the hell he was thinking, moves our boat right under the tree. The damn snake is straight above my head. If I look up, I can see his beady eyes looking back. If I reach up, I'm sure I can touch the critter.

For one of the very few times in my life, I am speechless. I am frozen into silence. While camera shutters click all around me, I scarcely breathe. I wonder if it is a constrictor or poisonous. I don't dare ask, for fear of annoying the snake. When our driver finally starts the motor and moves away from the tree, I release the air from my lungs. However, I don't speak for a very long time. The highlight hasn't been seeing the snake in its natural habitat... it is no longer seeing it at all.

After an approximate two hours on the river, we arrive at our eco-lodge, which is rather rustic, similar to a summer camp setting, constructed out of local, natural materials. Here the next bit of trouble begins. Everyone is led to his or her room, that is everyone except another woman, Janet, and I, who, before signing up for the tour, requested and have been promised single rooms.

"Sorry, we have no rooms for you."

"But…but reservations were made over a month ago."

"Yes, sorry, but we have no other rooms available today. Unless you want to move into someone else's room. We will have room tomorrow."

What? No room at the inn? Do I look like the Virgin Mary? There are no mangers here. Do I look like I want to sleep in the jungle?

"Sorry, I'm not sharing," Janet insists, "you must find rooms for us. These reservations were made some time ago, and we paid our deposits then."

"We have no singles available. You need to share."

"I'm not sharing either," I persevere, "I snore. I wouldn't do that to anyone else." Under my breath, I mutter to Janet, "It's obvious. They have overbooked."

Before the situation turns violent, and it hovers on that precipice, our guide's assistant suggests, "Leave the problem with us; we will resolve it one way or another."

She and the lodge management wander off, heads together in discussion. When they return, after several minutes have passed, the assistant informs us, "They are going to open two rooms in another building that is currently under renovation. But they have to be cleaned first. Just wait here until they are ready."

So while our fellow travellers rest and refresh themselves, we wait in the lobby. Wait and wait and wait. A couple of hours later, we are led to our rooms, some distance from the main lodge, but connected with boardwalk.

The rooms are shabby. Cobwebs hang from the doorways. It appears the floor hasn't been swept. Cleanliness is questionable. Huge holes characterize the mosquito netting. But they have beds, with fresh bedding, and clean towels. We will manage for one night.

Besides that, there is a welcoming committee of sorts. I go into the bathroom, not expecting company. On the back of the toilet tank, there is an enormous frog... all I can see are two feet gripping the tank, and his head, with huge eyes and what appears to be a wide smile. His body is behind the tank. He doesn't move. He looks like one of those rubber toys that can be clamped on to things. I reach to touch him and he ducks down behind the tank.

Now I know there are poisonous frogs in the Amazon, and although he is a very handsome frog who seems friendly, I'm not keen on dying in my sleep. I call the guide who has carried my luggage and is still nearby, and lead him to the bathroom. He can see the frog hanging on to the back of the tank.

"He's here alright," he says.

"Is he dangerous?" I inquire.

"I don't think so. But I will get someone from the hotel to take him out."

The guide disappears. By the time he returns with a staff member, the frog has vanished. We check under the bed, on shelves, in the shower, and in other potential frog hiding places. He is nowhere to be found. I am a little disappointed. I wish I had photographed him. I am also pleased, however, that he made a clean getaway, probably through one of the wider cracks in the rather rustic board floor.

In the late afternoon, we leave by boat for the 'lagoon' (laguna), a swimming hole where several boats congregate to watch sunset. Boats 'park' alongside a narrow strip of land extending into the water. A number of young guys play soccer. Swimmers are in the water on both

138

sides of the land. And, a caiman lurks nearby the opposite shore. I can't believe it! Do soccer players and swimmers not see the caiman? Do they not realize it has big teeth? Is a carnivore? A carnivore that may be hungry? At any rate, they pay no attention. Swimmers pass by, soccer players yank the ball out of nearby waters. At one point, I think the ball is going to hit the caiman on the head.

"Aren't you going swimming?" one of my fellow travellers encourages.

"Hell, no, do you think I'm crazy? I'm staying on the boat, not sticking even a toe in that water. In spite of my complaints about their age and appearance, I still like my body parts too much to sacrifice them."

Time approaches sunset. A number of boats are loaded and speed off. One last swimmer emerges, dries off, clambers into our boat. He isn't there thirty seconds when a caiman surfaces at the very spot where he was swimming.

After the sun dips beneath the horizon, we go 'caiman hunting', if you can imagine. Who wants to caiman hunt? And what happens when we find one? Our guide shines his spotlight along the shore, and several times, red eyes peer back. The light seems to mesmerize them. Sometimes our boat 'driver' takes us closer to shore to observe, but thankfully, no one is keen about catching a caiman to provide opportunity for a close-up view. Or for caiman stew.

Boating on the river in the coolness of night is rather marvelous. There is no moon, but a million stars light the darkened sky, more than I have seen since I was a child. The boat drivers seem to have a sixth sense, familiar with every curve of the river, aware of fallen tree branches in the black river. The harmony of frogs and cicadas in concert is our symphony.

We awake to gorgeous sunshine, threatening another hot day. It is cooler on the river, with much of it shadowed by tropical rainforest, including palms, macrolobiums, philodendrons and orchids. No tapir, deer, jaguar or pumas, which hunt at night, but several types of birds, macaws, herons and egrets, spectacled owl, kingfishers, eagles, vultures, (and others whose names have slipped away) frequent the shoreline. Grey and pink river dolphins fish the waters, gracefully arching and cavorting nearby. Iridescent blue Morpho butterflies flit around us. We also see more monkeys, turtles, a boa constrictor, thankfully not overhead, small lizards, large beetles and termite nests. We have experienced the peaceful magic of the Amazon jungle.

A visit to an indigenous village is scheduled for the last afternoon. Five Indian groups live nearby: Cofan, Secoya, Siona (Sioni), Quichua, and Achuar (Shuar). The Huaorani (Warani) and Yawepare have retreated deep into the jungle, subsequent to oil drilling and its devastating effects upon the land, and have much less interface with the outside world.

Our visit is with a Sioni shaman and his wife. We hoist ourselves from the boat onto a high dock and struggle up a bank, sufficiently steep to discourage unwanted visitors. We are greeted at a large community structure with a thatched roof, benches, and several pieces of unfamiliar tools. A smoking fire keeps mosquitoes at bay. This is a large cooking facility, which we understand is commonly separate from living quarters.

The rapport that exists between the guide and the Shioni is apparent and admirable. We are told the indigenous in this area are largely self-sufficient, relying upon fishing, farming and hunting, the last of which takes men away from their communities for days at a time. The news that they drink river water, much of which seems to be polluted, is alarming. They apparently travel by boat to 'outside' communities to purchase staples such as gas, sugar and matches, little else, although a weed-eater lies in the nearby grass.

The woman leads us on a trek into the forest, where we come upon what would best be described as a 'yuca orchard' (as distinct from yucca). I would have never guessed that yuca plants somewhat resemble shrubs or small trees; I would have surmised them to be low to the ground, more like turnips or sweet potatoes. Nevertheless, she is careful in choosing a particular 'tree', uproots it, revealing huge, starchy, tuberous roots, also known as cassava. With a machete, and a few strokes, she whacks off the outer skin as easily as peeling a banana. When she has retrieved half a dozen roots, more or less, she breaks a piece of branch and plants it in the hole left by the plant she removed. In three months, a new yuca plant will be ready for harvest. Sustainability at its best.

Back at the village hut, the yuca root, high in carbohydrates, is cleaned, chopped, grated and pounded into fine flour that is pressed on a metal pan over the fire. In a mere few minutes, yuca bread, resembling a dry tortilla, is ready for sampling. We are told it is a staple of the Sioni, both in the village and on hunting trips. We are also given a taste of a strong fermented yuca brew, similar to chicha. We all drink from the same gourd; the thought of contagious diseases briefly flicks through my mind but disappears when the fire of the brew burns my tongue. Germs would never survive this concoction.

A diet of yuca is supplemented with worms and grubs, snake, monkey, caiman, piranha, and in some cases, ants. I feel grateful our food at the resort has been somewhat nondescript, and that I can easily identify all of the foodstuffs without becoming squirmish. Everyone knows I am a 'foodie', but these critters haven't exactly made my list of exotic delicacies that must be sampled.

The shaman meets with us, explains through an interpreter, his role as a medium to bridge human and spiritual worlds, a healer. The offspring of shamans frequently prepare for a number of years to become shamans themselves. They are extremely knowledgeable about botanicals and medicinal herbs and plants.

After conducting a small ceremony to free each of us from negative energy and instill positive energy, he demonstrates the use of a blow gun, which shoots poison darts, for hunting purposes. He aims and hits bull's eye, from several meters distant. Our turn is next. A few of us are right on or near target. As for me, let it suffice to say, in spite of trying twice, the Sioni won't be taking me hunting any time soon.

On the river, for the last time, as we leave Cuyabeno Forest Reserve, I think about what has transpired over the past few days. But it is not the Reventador, vehicle breakdown, Lago Agrio, or the fiasco over rooms that occupy my thoughts. Neither is it the spectacular Antisana Ecological Reserve, which we will visit on the return trip to see condors flying in the wild, nor the nearby Fallarones of Isco, an extraordinary landscape where waves of lava erupted from the earth instead of a crater. Rather, I ponder the creatures and humans who inhabit this precious rainforest, interruptions to their lives, and recent invasions to their connection with the land. Never before has the ecological footprint we leave upon the earth been so personally meaningful. Once again in my travels, I have met myself along the way.

PIERRE'S NEMESIS

*"A friend is one to whom one may pour out all the contents
of one's heart, chaff and grain together, knowing that the
gentlest of hands will take and sift it, keep what is worth
keeping and with a breath of kindness blow the rest away."*

Arabian Proverb

Slouched at the Mill House beachfront bar, where
they have been since mid-morning, are Pierre and Duncan,
Canadians who several years previous, craving beer and
burgers, anchored their sailboat at Sint Eustatius, an island
in the Caribbean Dutch Antilles. They never left. Pierre,
quite a 'hunk', thirty-something, tall, tanned, bearded, lanky
but muscular, sits hunched on a rattan stool, nursing a
Heineken, elbows on the counter. He holds his dark, wavy-
haired head in both hands, as though it hurts, and makes eye
contact with no one. It is now late afternoon.

Duncan, slightly older, gnome-like, short and
stocky with a ruddy complexion and reddish-tinged, curly,
frizzy hair and beard, is standing nearby, reading a three-
month-old Macleans, throwing back yet one more Scotch,
straight up. That he can read let alone comprehend is a
marvel. In fact, that he is still standing is a miracle.

****

During several visits to the island I became well
acquainted with these two guys. Became rather fond of
them, in fact. Frequently, they asked me to bring them
something 'truly Canadian' when I returned. Once, I

143

presented to Duncan, encased in elegant black velvet, a Canadian-made pendant, an eye-catching 'Thompson (Manitoba) gold nugget' on a leather thong.

"Very attractive," he whistles under his breath. "What is it?" he asked.

"A moose turd," I say.

With a clunk it hits the table, bounces.

"Preserved in a chemical solution of some sort, then shellacked," I add. He cocks his head, raises his eyebrows, wags a threatening finger.

"You wanted authentic Canadian," I say. "You got authentic. You can't deny that."

"Right," he smirks, "but I'll remember this."

Another time, I smuggled in a sirloin tip roast of Canadian beef for the 'guys'. Hell, they were always complaining about the toughness of Argentine beef. I froze the meat, meticulously sealed it in plastic wrap, newspaper, and beach towel, clandestinely transported it, shrouded in clothing, in my suitcase. A terrific idea, or at least I thought so at the time. Nothing else could be more Canadian. Nothing else would be more appreciated. I was rather proud.

That is until my luggage went astray! It was the only time in my life that my luggage was lost, at least until this point in time. What can I say? I arrived in Sint Maarten. No luggage. Onward to Sint Eustatius the next day. No luggage. I mean what does one do? But file a complaint, purchase a few pieces of clothing, and wait, and wait and wait... chewing my nails. Which normally I don't do.

On the fourth day, after three restless nights, at 11:23 am, I was summoned to the hotel lobby. My luggage had arrived, I was told. I should come immediately, I was told. Okay, I think, this vacation is over. I wonder what the jail in St. Eustatius or St. Maarten is like? I wonder where I will be shipped from there? I wonder if they will let me change from my bikini and lacy cover-up into something more appropriate for a police station? I have witnessed the governor's inauguration on the island. Including the rather poorly organized and pathetic parade that followed. I hope this is a good sign.

Dragging myself to the foyer I hesitate, peer through potted palm fronds near the entrance, expect to see a forlorn, abandoned suitcase dripping blood, swarming with flies, alongside customs police. No one. No immigration officials. No police. Only my relatively unscathed suitcase. I creep gingerly toward it. One step at a time. Wait to see if lurking officials pounce once I have recovered it. Scan the area to detect hidden cameras.

No one is visible. Nothing heard. Or discerned. I sneak forward, grab the suitcase like a starving street person might a big Mac, drag it to my room in a time clocked only by Donavon Bailey in the 100 meter (a decision I believe contributed to subsequent cervical spine deterioration), plop it on the floor. Take a deep breath. Maybe the room is bugged. Maybe more hidden cameras. I circle the suitcase, eyeing it as one might a grenade with the potential to explode. A shot of rum later (if I am going to prison it may be best I am in a laissez-faire state), I dare to insert the key into the suitcase lock. Open it slowly. Nothing. I unwrap the towel. The roast is still there. It was apparently flying between cities in below-freezing cargo holds, and is just beginning to thaw. The following day, Pierre and Duncan host a feast to celebrate the end of my smuggling career.

****

Now, slipping into sandals, my current companion and I saunter from the black sand beach onto the slab-stoned beachfront terrace for what had become a daily ritual, joining locals and hotel guests for early pre-dinner drinks,

145

exchanging tales, scanning the horizon for the elusive green spot (the rarely-observed green flash that occurs in this part of the world, a second after the sun drops below the horizon).

In spite of our camaraderie, although Duncan turns, waves, grins from ear to ear, Pierre doesn't respond to our greeting. We understand. Last night's bash, hosted for several disembarked cruise boat guests, lies unspoken in the space between us, smoulders like a huge, red-hot iron, one none of us wants to touch.

****

Fortunately or unfortunately, depending on one's perspective, the barbequed burgers aren't the only thing sizzling. After dinner, the action moves to the terrace where scantily clad bodies gyrate to bongos, and more drinks are poured than at a Governor General's New Year's levee. As the noise and frenzy escalates, many hotel guests retire to their rooms, to enjoy a nightcap from beachfront balconies. Hell, let me be honest, most consider themselves better 'voyeurs' than participants in these festivities.

Sometime later, after the band has packed up and left, after the shuttle boat has already returned the cruisers to their ship, Pierre, in cut-offs, barefoot and shirtless, stumbles on to the beach below. Equally unsteady, hanging precariously on his arm, staggers a voluptuous curly-haired blonde, in skintight white shorts and a strapless red-striped tee that exposes a considerable portion of her ample breasts. Pierre collapses on the sand, lies inert, unmoving. Wasting no time, she begins to disrobe him, then herself, in the light of the moon, and in the full view of spectators, both in the bar and on balconies.

One might conclude this gal is no novice at this sort of thing. However, at this point, it is time to turn away, draw the drapes. The invasion of their privacy in this manner, especially Pierre's, is too much to bear. For some time before silence befalls the beach, however, observers can be heard clapping and cheering.

At any rate, early this morning, the patio overflows with guests and islanders chattering, lingering over breakfast, waiting for Pierre to appear. The story is that, when the ship couldn't account for all its passengers, a few brawny crewmen returned and carted the near-comatose but still-smiling woman to the shuttle boat. However, no one seems to know when or how Pierre, so totally intoxicated, managed to get up and proceed home. In fact, no one seems to understand how he managed to 'get it up' either.

When, sometime around ten, he shuffles in, nursing the hangover of the century, the crowd breaks into applause, claps, whistles, cheers, not unlike the ovation during the previous night's performance. He scans the room, startled, perplexed, befuddled, shakes his head as though to rid it of cobwebs that have lodged without invitation. Duncan has been assigned the task of enlightening Pierre on the previous night's activity, as quietly and gently and subtly as is possible amidst taunts and guffaws. As comprehension penetrates his fog, Pierre freezes, groans, covers his eyes, orders a beer, perhaps to forget, perhaps to still jangling nerves, perhaps for courage, then slumps in humiliation at the bar where he has since remained consuming one Heineken after another.

We decide to let him be; we will wait until he is ready to face us, look us in the eye. Sometimes life circumstances are such that consolation, solace can only come from within. One has to reach, grasp it for oneself. Sometimes it is necessary to be alone in order to tap inner strength, to draw on resources that rarely disappoint. To summon whatever courage we need to once again reach out to others.

Instead, we greet Isabella, a skinny, hawk-nosed, angular-featured, stereotypical, over-protective New York Jewish mama, whose grey frizz gives her the appearance of having stuck her finger in an electrical socket. She somewhat resembles Albert Einstein in drag. Without a word of a lie, my own hair pales in comparison. She is travelling with her slightly balding son and his grey-haired gay lover who, for the first time in the past week, are not by her side. She has an untouched glass of red wine at her elbow.

"Have you seen Saulie and Mel?" she whines, wringing her hands. "They went up the Quill (an inactive volcanic cone) this morning and something must have happened to them because they aren't back yet and I'm worried sick that they got hurt or something and I don't understand how they could leave me alone all day like this but surely they must be hurt or something or they would be back by now." She pauses for breath.

"I'm sure they are fine," I reply, slightly turning my head so she won't see my eyes rolling upward to my hairline. "It takes an entire day to explore the Quill, and they are likely waiting until it is cooler for the walk back."

"Oh, my dear no. They should be here by now and I cannot believe they are not and I am so worried. How could they do this to me? Someone must go search for them. Do you know who might go? How could they do this? They know I worry so about them." She continues to spew on and on. I admire her ability in this regard.

At first opportunity my companion reassures her, "Just wait. You'll see. They'll be back soon. They'll be fine."

Just then, Donna and Mark, a pleasant American couple who arrived just this afternoon, step onto the terrace, greet the others, move off to a side table, trying to gain some semblance of privacy.

She turns toward them, "Have you seen Saulie and Mel? They must be hurt, they went to climb the mountain this morning and haven't returned and how could they leave me all alone, how could they...." She babbles onward.

I continue biting my tongue to prevent it from expelling thoughts beyond my conscious capability. My companion throws a warning glance in my direction.

We scoop up our drinks, turn toward the sunset. Good for the guys, I silently muse, their first chance to be alone in a week. Perhaps they'll stay out all night. Perhaps they've returned to New York. Perhaps they've moved to Timbuktu. Under the circumstances, all of these options would certainly be tempting. On second thought, those possibilities frighten me. Who will deal with her, who will calm her, cater to her whims until she can be loaded on a plane? Who will meet her plane? Such a tragedy. New York will never be the same.

Shortly thereafter, appearing cool and refreshed, Saul in a white and navy-striped caftan and Mel, in sharply creased grey trousers and an open-necked white shirt, arrive. They are both smiling. Briefly.

"Oh my, oh my," gasps Isabella. Her hand clasps her throat. She directs her comments to Saulie, totally ignores Mel. "You are here, finally, safe and sound. I am so pleased. I was so, so worried, you have no idea... I had already arranged a search party... I told everyone you must be hurt or you would never have left me alone all day, especially knowing I have a heart condition... this isn't like you... I said something must have happened because you are always so kind and just wouldn't ever be this cruel... unless something terrible happened... oh my this is such a shock to see you..."

She clutches her bosom, puffing and wheezing, as her son moves toward her, murmuring concern, offering consolation. We swing around to see if she is alright.

That is when it happens. I swear it wasn't intentional. I turn, bump into the waiter who, unbeknown, is passing directly behind with a tray of drinks. The ice bucket catapults cubes across Isabella's table, into her lap. That isn't quite all. A cold Heineken pours down her back. That isn't quite all. A Singapore Sling sloshes over her head, stranding an orange slice and cherry in her frizzy coiffure. That is all.

Isabella shrieks, yowls. Wails like a dying cat in heat. Understandably so. She leaps to her feet, cursing, berating, beating the air with her fists. Understandably so. Perhaps.

Saul throws an arm around her shoulders, "Are you alright mother? Mother?" She moans and, her knees slowly buckling beneath her, slides to the floor. I swear as the others, like clucking hens, gather around her. I swear one of her eyes opens, slightly, briefly, as she smiles, an ever-so-slight smirk.

Mark identifies himself as a doctor, leans over Isabella, checks her pulse, then her heartbeat with the stethoscope his wife has rapidly retrieved from his satchel. He reassures concerned spectators, "She is fine. She will be just fine."

She opens her eyes, peers around as though dazed, as though she has awakened from a deep and lengthy coma. She groans, grasps her son's hand.

"Mother, this is a doctor. He says you will be fine. Perhaps you want to lie down for a while. I will stay with you to be certain."

The corners of Isabella's mouth turn up. "Oh yes," she murmurs, "that is wise."

"Oh no," Mark jumps in, "She must be hospitalized, more thoroughly checked. At the very least she should be observed overnight, kept away from stress or excitement."

"Of course, she must."

She begins to sputter. She shakes her head like one might a dust mop, or like a dog emerging from the sea. Shakes her head in vain.

"Mother, you heard the doctor and I insist. It would be foolish to ignore the doctor's advice. You must go, that's all there is to it."

Saul and Mark prop her up between them, lead her to the waiting ambulance. Isabella is no longer smiling. Saul and Mel, however, exchanging glances, may well be suppressing theirs. It takes everything in me to stifle mine.

The drama is over. We approach the bar to refresh our rum.

Duncan winks, grins, mutters under his breath, raises his glass "Perfect timing. To moose turds and roast beef, eh?"

Pierre faces us squarely, sheepishly grimaces, "Thank god I'm not the only one who makes an ass of himself."

I grin in his direction, "Yes, we all have our moments, don't we?"

He beams, raises his glass. We click glasses.

I know then Pierre will be okay. So will I. And Duncan. Our friendship will survive. Those who weather rough seas together, face frailties, share vulnerabilities and accept imperfections, defend honour and are still able to laugh together are friends worth keeping.

Sheila Carnegie

ESMERELDA VISITS VIETNAM

"Friends are the most important part of your life. Treasure the tears, treasure the laughter, but most importantly, treasure the memories."

Dave Brenner

I haven't the slightest idea what prompted me to go to Vietnam, of all places. Maybe it was because I was tired of hearing friends rave about their trips to that part of the world. Or maybe I needed an adventure. Or perhaps Sheila's spirit guides cajoled me in that direction. Whatever, here I am, in the Paris airport, awaiting a flight to Hanoi.

I have deliberately chosen a route through Bogota and Paris. Hell, after that trip to Esmeraldas with Sheila, and all her hassles with US Immigration, I avoid going through the States, in event that her reputation has tainted mine. And I am hesitant to fly through Mexico City to make connections. I could be arrested on the spot. I mean it wasn't just that mess I got into in the dress shop, or even the *dulces de coco*. There was a third episode with Mexican's finest. Come to think of it, I haven't yet told anyone about that. At any rate, better I not cross the border into Mexico. I have no history in Colombia or Paris. At least not yet.

The airline gate, which has already been changed twice, is some distance from where the trolley dropped me. I didn't mind the walk though. I had plenty of time to browse through a few shops along the way, not that I could afford to buy anything. Hell, I can't imagine paying 250 Euros for a silk scarf, let alone 2500 Euros for a rainbow-coloured dress that features more 'bling' than the Aurora

Borealis, and barely covers boobs and butt. Actually looks more like a bathing suit, if you ask me. Dee might be interested, but I'll wait for silk shops in Vietnam, thank you very much.

A shadow falls over my magazine. "Madam, Hanoi?" queries a flat-faced, olive-skinned woman with long, straight, black hair and almond-shaped, dark eyes.

"Yes, Hanoi." I point to the flight notice beside the desk. She is Asian, and appears lost. Perhaps she cannot read.

"Hanoi? Hanoi?"

"Yes, Hanoi," I reassure, nodding vehemently.

"Madam, Hanoi? Hanoi?" she repeats. I'm not sure why she chooses me. I resemble neither the airline receptionist nor any of the stewardesses waiting nearby, come to think of it, no one likely to be from Hanoi. Perhaps, she believes my age is an assurance of wisdom?

"Do you live in Hanoi?" I ask.

"No speaking English," she replies. "Hanoi?" she repeats.

"Yes, Hanoi." I point again to the flight sign.

"Hanoi." She nods, seemingly satisfied, and plops into the empty seat beside me. Perhaps she was waiting for an invitation. Perhaps she had a motive about which I know nothing. I silently hope she doesn't have the seat next to me on the plane. I silently hope this isn't a sign of the cultural displacement I am about to face in a strange continent with languages I do not understand. God forbid this should be another fiasco like Mexico.

First Impressions: Hanoi

The plane lands in Hanoi at daybreak. Luggage retrieval and passage through immigration are as uneventful as the flight itself. The hotel has sent a car and after visually searching the crowd, I spot a slight, slim young fellow waving a card with my name on it. Good thing I didn't rely upon a physical description. Practically everyone in the airport is incredibly small and slender with dark hair. By the time we reach the hotel, thirty minutes later, culture shock has whacked me between the eyes with the unexpected force of a typhoon.

Initially, I blame my discombobulation on rush hour traffic. However, I am soon to learn that the noise, pollution, and traffic patterns are pretty much characteristic of Hanoi at any time of day and most of the night. Cars, huge trucks, and motorcycles monopolize highways and streets, weave in and out at high speeds, cross lanes without signaling, incessantly beep their horns, and never stop for pedestrians. One frequently sees half a dozen motorcycles (motos) abreast across two lanes, some carrying several people, including families of four or five, others toting huge live or butchered pigs, loads of flowers, trees, huge cartons, bags of produce, or just about anything one can imagine. Hell, one could carry a bundled dead body this way... or perhaps someone already is.

Hundreds of billboards and signs cover buildings and line streets. Vocabulary consists of words such as hung, sung, dung, rang, kang, sang, fang, gang, bang, dam, lam, sam, nam, tram, cong, dong, bong, thoung, troung, khaong, some of which are stuck together in various combinations with others. Included are phe, phi, pho, though no phum, but I do see a phooee. Many of them are accented, and one word can be accented in several different manners. If you can believe it, even the local currency is called 'dong'. I wonder if there is a 'ding-dong'.

By the time we arrive at the hotel my head is swimming. To enter, my driver and I must walk on the street, around a barrier of motorcycles perpendicularly parked on the sidewalk. They will remain there all day. A welcoming receptionist, elegantly attired in a typical scarlet and gold long silk tunic, worn over pants ('ao dai'), quickly escorts me to the restaurant for a hot breakfast, American style, to ward off the crisp December air. I gratefully accept; I will have plenty of time to sample local cuisine and specialties.

I pick up the teabag wrapper. The only word I can decipher is 'Vietnam'. I study the front, read about half way down, "Tra cúa mói gia dinh. S'an phám vá thuong hieu c'ua: Cong ty tnhh thu'o'ng mai vá dich vu bai gia...". I turn to the back, "Cách dung: Cho túi trá Vào Cốc dó kháong 80-100 ml núdc soi, Tuý theo s'o troung đậm, nhat, Nhúng khoáng 2 phút, có thé thém duóng, dá lanh tuy theo so' thích roi uóng..." (and I haven't even written that correctly; there are many other accents and curlicues my computer fails to print). I return the teabag to the saucer. There and then I make a decision. I will not learn to speak Vietnamese. I will not be in the country a sufficient length of time to learn this language. Hell, I will not live long enough to learn this language. I decide to concentrate on hello, please and thank you. That will be my linguistic goal for the next two months.

I sink beneath thick, silky comforters in a back bedroom and, to the muffled din of outside traffic, soon find refuge from encroaching jet lag. After several hours, I awaken, freshen up, and ask directions to Hồ Hoàn Kiếm Sword lake. According to legend, this famous Hanoi landmark houses giant turtles, and is about eight blocks from the hotel. The sun has cleared away early morning smog and warmed the midday air.

However, traffic remains frenetic, cars, trucks, motorcycles, tuk-tuks, bicycles, push carts filled with dishes, pots, fruits and vegetables, flowers, china, pots and pans, clothing and shoes, and so forth. There are neither traffic lights nor crosswalks. On narrow streets, i wait for a break in traffic and then run like hell. Wider streets have me baffled. I step onto the pavement. A horn blares, and one motorcycle almost slices my toes while another whips behind me. I feel air rush up my jeans. My head swivels rapidly, seeking a lull in the traffic. A second, third, fourth try. No dice. Finally, there is a sufficient opening to actually make it a quarter of the way. Vehicles and motos, horns blowing, whizz by me on both sides. I am stuck in the street. an older Vietnamese gentleman holds up one hand in warning to oncoming vehicles, rushes to my side and takes my arm. He again signals traffic and escorts me to the other side. I am soon to learn that his kindness, helpfulness, and generosity of spirit, are typical of the Vietnamese people. I have learned my first Vietnamese word. *Cảm ơn. Thank you.*

In a restaurant near the lake, a plate of Bún Chả, vermicelli noodles with pork meatballs, beansprouts, greens, and cucumbers, and a cup of Vietnamese iced coffee sweetened with condensed milk, are comforting. They somewhat compensate for the absence of turtle sightings. Instead, for some time, I watch people, obviously scurrying in one direction or another. Caucasians have no exclusivity on the Protestant work ethic.

On my return to the hotel, I snap photos and wander through shops, which have been colourfully decorated in preparation for forthcoming New Year celebrations. By the time I reach the hotel, prompted by a developing headache,

I've made a second decision. Hanoi isn't for me. The constantly swirling stimuli are overwhelming, though I hate to admit it. What would be Dee's heaven is more like my hell.

Sea of Tranquility and Industry: Halong Bay

By noon the next day, I am lounging on a small cruise boat, floating around Halong Bay in morning mists, soaking up scarlet sunrises and blood-red sunsets, gorging on fresh seafood and tropical fruits, sipping cold fruit juice or Vietnamese beer, and musing about the new and strange world around me. Being lazy. Though I prefer to think of it as recovering from jetlag. I'm quite certain this will take several days.

The third day, cruise boat passengers transfer to small wooden boats, each rowed by a young Vietnamese woman, immaculately clad. Hell, all of them are young, slender, beautiful, stoic and diligent. The long, wooden, double-oars slice silent ocean water, and we move out of the bay further inland, where exists a village of house boats, varied in size, shape, style and colour, personalized as one might a private home. Some entrances are guarded by well-fed dogs; they, as I am to later learn, may have been food sources rather than pets or guard dogs. Most boats have lines strung across the deck where, in typical fashion of many Vietnamese homes, the family wardrobe is hung. As we pass through the 'village', and observe boats carrying provisions or kids rowing off to school, the hardship of life here becomes apparent.

I am impressed, as I had been in Hanoi, by the industriousness of the Vietnamese people. Everyone, regardless of age, seems to be working at something. Here it is fishing, pearl farming, tourism, food transportation, or hospitality services. Elsewhere, as I will learn over the next several weeks, it may be textiles, weaving, tailoring, stone and marble carving, intricate woodwork, lacquerware, origami, glasswork, metal sculpture, paintings, gold work, agriculture, manufacture and marketing, food preparation and sales, business of all types. There seem to be no free rides here. Those of retirement age certainly do not 'retire'. I must remember that next time I am counting my lucky stars.

Ancient Places: Hoi An, Hue, and My Son

Onward to Hoi An, an anagram of Hanoi, which seems to me another example of the strange language. Is there an Oi han, or a Noi ha? Hoi An, in Central Vietnam, was established as a South-East Asian trading port at the estuary of the Thu Bón River in the 1500's, and was subsequently settled by the Chinese, Japanese, Portuguese, Dutch and East Indians. Its site has been traced back to the 2nd century, and from the 4th to 13th was used as the commercial center of the Cham people, who controlled the spice trade.

Today, Hoi An is recognized as a UNESCO World Heritage Site, and is known for its long-established silk industry, and its well-preserved architecture, including pagodas, temples, restored homes, and a 16th – 17th century 'Japanese Bridge', the only existing covered bridge harbouring a Buddhist temple.

What draws me, however, even more than the prospect of a new wardrobe, is the Lantern Festival that occurs on the January full moon. The thought of dancing on moonlit streets adjacent to the river, brilliant with reflecting lights from thousands of handmade lanterns and floating candles, is irresistible.

While I am waiting for this event, several nearby spectacular historical and cultural attractions beckon. The first of these is My Son, a Hindu spiritual center of the Champu Kingdom, currently a UNESCO archaeological marvel that spanned centuries and civilizations. Subsequent to a week of 'carpet bombing' during the 'Vietnam War', or as the Vietnamese would say, the 'American War', only a handful of the approximate seventy temples and stone monuments bearing Sanskrit and Cham inscriptions remain. I wander among sacred ruins and bomb craters, contemplating the willingness of humanity to both create and destroy. I am in awe of this strangely silent and peaceful place. Had I known then, however, that in all probability unexploded shells remain in the vicinity, I doubt I would have questioned the tranquility.

The second major attraction was a UNESCO World Heritage site at Hue. The Imperial City (Forbidden City), a vast walled area ringed by a moat, encompassed four citadels and several palaces and shrines, including the Imperial Palace. The national capital, constructed after 1804 and controlled by feudal lords of the Nguyen dynasty, served as the political, cultural and religious center until 1945. Although only ten of the original 160 buildings escaped military decimation, the obvious luxuriant landscaping, architecture, furnishings and clothing are both impressive and inspiring.

Back in Hoi An, motivated by opulence of Nguyen kings, I frequent silk shops, and there are many. I soon learn I can purchase nothing off the racks. Even the XL garments get stuck on my head. These people are so tiny; I feel like a corpulent giant. Oh darn, I am compelled to order tailor-made. Most shops display samples and pattern catalogues. And they eagerly bargain prices. So in ensuing days, I have a 'shopping ball'. Thankfully, Dee isn't here to direct my choices.

Chattering shop clerks suggest styles and fabrics and colours. Of course, I have no idea what they're saying. It could be "this one looks like a pushover," or "she'd look terrible in yellow," or "god, can you believe her size?" However, we smile and nod and gesture a great deal and seem to be having an amiable time. By the time I leave Hoi An, my luggage is stuffed with silk. What troubles me, only a little, mind you, is that most garments, identical to elegant shop models, appear rather dumpling-like on me. However, the bigger concern is that I won't live long enough to wear all of them.

Making Lemonade From Lemons: Dalat

One cannot be in Vietnam and not notice the effects of war unless one is blind, self-absorbed or unconscious. However, as you may know, I prefer the lighter side of life. My friend, Sheila, is more likely to write about serious matters, and I will leave it to her to tell the horror stories. I agree with her that there is little, if any, humour to be found in war. In this instance, though, positive outcomes are impressive.

In Dalat, where American troops established a base, several locals are more-or-less fluent in English. However, no one speaks of the war. It's as though, for the sake of healing the community, no one dares. Rather like a family who buries its skeletons for the sake of survival. Here it is common knowledge that forests were destroyed and soil contaminated by the heavy use of napalm and agent orange. Yet, the Vietnamese have found ways to move ahead, to establish a productive economy, to survive.

Dalat, located in an area of natural beauty, is promoted, through a biannual Festival and otherwise, as both the 'City of Flowers' and a honeymoon destination. Flowers, which can be grown where vegetables cannot, are shipped to various parts of Vietnam and exported internationally. A huge floral park is gated with massive, sculpted dragons; tiered gardens offer themes, a cacophony of colour, and three-dimensional stories of Vietnamese life. My black thumb personally favours the succulent garden.

Tourism has also been developed in Dalat. Here roam the Easy Riders, motorcycle geniuses past their prime; wartime dispatchers turned tourist guides. At breakneck speed, they whizz about, enveloped by dust clouds, which leave one sneezing and choking. Their familiarity with sites and history render them exceptional guides, and they offer information, options and suggestions. Of course, they expect to be financially rewarded in accordance with time and effort expended, but no matter. They are interesting characters and know what they're doing.

In one of the 'home-stays' (similar to B & B's), I meet Jessica, an Australian author, and Margie, an American psychologist. The three of us are a perfect match, complementing each other, but similar in terms of ideas (all brilliant of course), risk-taking, and off-the-wall plans, which seem more or less normal to us. We frequently hang out together, laugh at ourselves, or at unexpected situations. Jessica sums it up, "Esmerelda dreams up stuff, Margie analyzes it, and I write about it."

We visit palaces, pagodas, museums, gardens, and indigenous villages. We ride a historic, local train to a mosaic temple site, and swing through the air on a creaking cable car across an incredible valley sheltering a brilliant blue lake shimmering with silver ribbon. A ride on a less-than-reliable rowboat ends only when our feet are soaked.

I fall in love with an architectural anomaly called the 'Crazy House' (go figure), shaped like a five-story banyan tree. A maze of 'theme' rooms are constructed of wire mesh, concrete and plaster, similar to adobe caves, and wrapped around huge tree roots emerging from the earth.

Rooms can be booked for short stays. The 'bear room' and 'tiger room', legitimized with genuine skins, are intriguing. However, with the exception of one room that is closed for viewing (I am still miffed... surely the honeymoon couple could have invited us in), my favorite is the 'condor', legendary transporter of souls to the heavens. I imagine how I could actually live here. Hell, when my number is up, I could hop on, and float away on widespread wings to my next adventure.

"Well, we could see if we could find you a husband here," offers Margie.

"No way. I don't want a husband," I object.

"It's not like you'd have to spend much time with him. There are so many rooms you could be on the run and rendezvous with him, well, maybe only at New Years, or his birthday," she replies.

"A woman built and owns this house," I retort.

"Well, surely she has sons or brothers or nephews, or cousins, or workers...."

"Okay, enough already. I gave up looking for a mate long ago."

At this point, Jessica pipes up, "Think of the potential. You could gather all sorts of stories and feed them to me, and we could sell magazine articles. And go on vacations with the income... it might even pay for our wine."

Chuckling, we all burst in at once, "Great idea!" "Terrific!" Wouldn't hurt to have a wine kitty." "Or a food kitty." They nod and laugh. Of course, that last comment was mine; they had quickly become familiar with my 'foodie' inclinations. We frequently ended the day at various restaurants, sampling 'hot pot' or 'bun cha' or 'ca khoto' (fish braised and carmelized in a clay pot), 'phó Báhn mi' (baguette stuffed with meatballs, fish or pork belly, pickled carrot and daikon), or other local and delicious delicacies such as steamed rice cakes and spring rolls. Naturally, dinner was usually accompanied by a bottle of wine. Margie always limited herself to one glass, albeit substantially sized; Jessica and I never had trouble polishing off the bottle.

The highlight of Dalat, however, is 'weasel coffee' (or civet coffee). Can you imagine? I have already learned that businesses in Asia often have weird English names, for example, Ruby True Hotel, Happy Money Massage, Lucky Sleep. And so forth. But weasel coffee? What the hell is that? Made from ground-up weasels? We have seen this listed on billboards and menus, and have noticed the price of this coffee is substantially higher than Vietnamese coffee. But none of us have any idea of what it is. So when an overly enthusiastic 'Easy Rider', determined to please, suggests we visit a coffee plantation, we cannot resist. I am more than curious. Well, believe it or not, we discover genuine 'weasel coffee'. In retrospect, it might have been better if we hadn't.

The motorcycle dips from the pavement and screeches to a stop so sudden it threatens to fling me over the driver's head onto the reddish earth. Jessica and Margie's drivers are not far behind. There ensues several minutes of sneezing through a dust cloud, a walkabout to regain balance and blood flow, and some deep-breathing in the washroom to overcome what I can only describe as 'petrifying fear' of being hurled over highway's edge into an abyss below, never to be found again. Reminds me of that bus ride in Mexico, which now seems like eons ago. Only this time I carry no rosary beads.

The 'weasel' coffee plantation, however, delivered as promised. We first viewed the coffee shrubs before we were introduced to the little 'weasels' (civets), which didn't at all resemble North American weasels, but seemed to be furry offshoots of what? Maybe small raccoons without the stripes? Or marmots? Mongoose? They were kind of cute and I was quite taken with them, that is, until I discovered their role in the whole process.

Now, honestly, no matter how liberal leaning you might consider yourself, you are going to have trouble believing this. Without a word of a lie, however, when coffee beans are ripe they are plucked or gathered from the ground, by diligent workers. Herein comes the hook. They are not processed as regular beans. They are fed to 'weasels', which gobble them up like a pig might truffles, and eventually pass them onward. Right. You got it. 'Weasel poop' is then dried and washed, so only the beans remain. Let it suffice to say that when we return to the attached restaurant to sample coffee produced by the plantation, we are strangely silent. None of us select 'weasel coffee', and I'd venture to say it had nothing to do with the price. Somehow the boundaries to our risk-taking had been established.

The irony is that the coffee plantation is situated on land that, in all probability, had been previously contaminated by agent orange. It could well be that 'weasel coffee' might actually be purified by weasel poop, and perhaps is healthier than non-weasel coffee. But what would that do to the weasels?

'Eggonomic' Development in the Mekong Delta

Towards the end of January, when Margie joins friends on the coast, Jessica and I decide to spend 'Tet', the Vietnamese New Year, in the south.

In Can Tho, preparations are underway. Several boats from the floating vegetable and fruit market have been moored. Others have become amazing golden yellow floating gardens. Onshore markets are bustling as provisions are gathered for family feasting, which will last for days. Small apricot blossom trees (hoa mai, which symbolize wealth, well-being, and passion), mickey mouse shrubs (ochna integerrima), and pots of chrysanthemums are being hand-carried or transported on bicycles and motos. We are told that the colour yellow is representative of noble roots.

It's the year of the horse, and everywhere there are magnificent golden floral horses, along with spectacular sculptures of dragons and just about everything one can imagine. Including a Pepsi sign (I have seen 'Coca-Cola' advertised in all parts of the world, but this may have been one time they were outdone). Stunning displays have been constructed from thousands and thousands of blooms, at least some of which have been imported from Dalat. Such breathtaking beauty is an experience to be treasured by everyone, except perhaps those with allergies or asthma.

From Can Tho we decide to tour an island in the Mekong Delta. We cross the river, change to two smaller canoe-like boats, each rowed by a woman, and float down a stream overhung with palm branches. Except for the sound of oars slicing water, it is perfectly silent. The slight cool breeze does little to still rivulets of sweat that search their way beneath my cotton clothing.

Here, as has been the case in previous explorations, industry is apparent. Island inhabitants have thought of various ways to generate income, fresh fruit, honey candy from local beehives, entertainment by a musical family. All is proceeding peacefully, that is, until the snake is brought in. I can't believe it... we can actually pet this snake? We can have this boa or python or whatever the hell it is perched around our shoulders so we can have a photo? And pay a small sum for the privilege of so doing??? I mean, how crazy do they think we are? Just as I am pondering this, the guide, who doesn't pay a cent, wraps the snake around him, rather like a fox collar, and offers it to another willing tourist (who is quite willing to pay). Question answered.

As if that wasn't enough, Jessica further exemplified irrationality of Caucasian tourists. Well, since she was from Australia, thank heavens it didn't reflect badly upon Canadians. It all started with a cockfight, or at least a planned cockfight. Two handsome specimens were carried out and placed at a distance in front of us. One 'chap' was rust-coloured with teal and orange highlights, and fine orange and black plumage around his neck. The other had variegated shades of black, brown, tan, and white, with some rust highlights and a black and white feathered tail.

They lowered their heads, tentatively approaching each other as though to assess the opponent. The feathers around their necks stood straight out. It seemed that at any moment one would attack the other. I looked toward the guide and shook my head vehemently. I have a sense of adventure but not an inclination toward the violent. I recognize threatening signals from some of my friends, former friends, that is. Sheila and I have that in common. Neither of us likes needless conflict; both of us view animals as living creatures that deserve abuse no more than humans; both of us abhor violence. Entertainment in the form of cock fighting, to my way of thinking, is both abusive and violent.

"Please, no." I implore the guide in no uncertain terms, and hold up my hands in protest. The guide speaks in Vietnamese to the 'cockfight promoter', who raises questioning eyebrows, slightly smiles, gathers one cock under his arm and disappears.

The second cock is strutting around as though he claimed victory by default. The owner eventually comes to claim him but, in the meantime, Jessica's admiration exceeds her common sense.

"What gorgeous creatures!" she sucks in her breath.

"Yes, they are," I reply. "So why would you want to see them bloodied, or worse yet dead?"

"Oh, I don't," she reassures me. "But I wouldn't mind taking one or two home with me; my male friend is quite interested in raising chickens."

"Now, how the hell can you take them home? In cages under your airplane seat? And what the hell will you do with them until then? If you haul them around Vietnam they are sure to be transformed into phó before morn."

"Well, I could take eggs home," she ponders, "in an unbreakable container in my luggage. They would be warm and safe there." She nods as though this is a done deal.

I suspect there is no point in trying to dissuade her. I am right. With her chin assertively jutted, she orders three chicken eggs, to be fertilized by three different roosters (how the hell is that to be guaranteed?), and picked up in a few days. She is determined to get them back to Australia.

I look away, head bowed, rub my hand across my face, try my damndest to communicate to these fine Vietnamese people that this is no idea of mine. However, the cock owner and guide look quite proud and pleased. Or maybe it is a cat-caught-the-canary expression, or an entirely new business idea.

Now, I have been accused of being eccentric, but it seems to me I am clearly outmatched by Jessica. We have six more weeks to travel, separately or together has yet to be decided. I mean, how long does it take an egg to hatch? I always thought it was twenty-some days? What happens if the eggs hatch along the way? What do we do with the chicks? What do you feed baby chicks that have no mothers? Or should I say have only human mothers? What happens if they hatch on a plane or in a bus somewhere? How do we keep the chicks warm? Or more importantly, quiet?

What happens if the eggs break? Isn't 'chick-slaughter' akin to manslaughter'? Or reckless endangerment? How will one dispose of the 'bodies'?

Doesn't Jessica need permits to take live creatures back into Australia? I know one cannot import animal products into Canada. I learned that when I tried to bring a baby pet iguana into the country from Mexico. Another fiasco I'd rather not discuss.

I am haunted by countless questions. I sound like Sheila the time we travelled to Esmeraldas. What has happened to my sense of adventure? Especially since *Horton Hatches the Egg* is my favourite Dr. Suess book.

When Jessica collects her nondescript eggs, I feign disinterest. These offspring will be her responsibility, not mine. Be damned if I am carrying eggs in my luggage wrapped in all that new silk. I refuse to become attached. As it turned out, we amicably parted ways a couple of weeks later, before the eggs hatched. Although we kept in touch for some time, I never did ask, nor did I hear about the fate of my recently conceived 'nieces and nephews'.

Hodge Podge: Ho Chi Minh City

Our next adventure is Ho Chi Minh City. At New Year's, festivities abound. Flowers are everywhere, even on the decks of shabby riverboats and derelict shacks. Streets are decorated with thousands of lights. Kumquat trees are commonly displayed, as are yellow blossoming apricot trees, adorned with red and gold baubles. Young people buy 'lucky money', lottery-like tickets or actual cash in red envelopes, for family and friends. I am told the gesture of 'doing so' will bring one good fortune. I contemplate buying one for Jessica, as an act of good faith, a blessing of sort for her egg embryos, but I let opportunity slide by. I hope my negligence won't come back to haunt me.

Tet celebrations last at least two to three weeks. Everyone goes 'home', to the place in Vietnam where they grew up, or where families remain. Most places of business are closed for three days to a week, in some cases as long as a month. The New Year's Eve sky is illuminated with massive fireworks enjoyed by thousands. Families, elegantly and beautifully attired, pack Central Park, on both New Years Day and days following, wandering among huge, spectacularly sculptured floral arrangements, chatting, sampling aromatic delights from small street side cookeries.

The national New Years dish in Vietnam is bánh tét (or bánh chu'ng), cakes of glutinous rice with mung bean paste and banana or pork, wrapped in banana leaves, meticulously tied, like small precious gifts, and steamed. They can be seen everywhere, including at New Year's Day breakfast. The hotel is extremely short-staffed for the holiday, but a huge buffet has been set out. It includes several soups, phó, the most common Vietnamese noodle soup, crab soup and congee, a variety of dumplings and rice dishes, wraps and spring rolls, prawns, fish, sliced pork cakes, grilled and chopped chicken, stewed meats, fermented sausages, cold cuts, breads and pastries, fresh and candied fruits with nuts.

I want to try everything, which is impossible, so I concentrate on both favourite and unfamiliar dishes. Back at my table, festively dressed in white linen, crystal and silver, I nibble a prawn dumpling, sample a bánh ch'ung, then dig my chopsticks into what appears to be a crunchy rice dish. Whoa!!!!! What is this? I remove my spectacles, closely peer into the concoction on my plate. Bad news... worms! Oh hell, yes, most definitely. Tiny, teeny worms, but worms just the same. Good news... they aren't moving. Not good enough though, I cannot convince myself to try them. I tell myself the beginning of a new year is a good time for a new adventure. It doesn't work. Am I losing my daring spirit?

I am reminded of a couple of weeks earlier in Dalat. I was determined to try an 'authentically genuine' Vietnamese restaurant and, after searching for some time, I was pointed in the right direction.

The room was very tiny, sparsely furnished with a few wooden tables and stools. The owner/manager quizzically raised his eyebrows. I was not to be deterred. He gestured toward glass cases that displayed the dishes; one could just point to what they wanted. Perfect. I remembered doing this in Greece, discovering fantastic food in fact. I approached the glass case, scrutinized each compartment one by one. Without a word of a lie, all of them were moving!!! Every single one! More or less, to one degree or another, but moving just the same. With one critter or another. Some of which I could not identify. I swallowed hard, placed my hands in a prayer-like position, bowed slightly and backed out. The owner bowed in return and smiled. So much for trying authentic cuisine.

Ho Chi Minh City is a mixed bag for me. Hot and humid. Crowded. Thousands of bodies weaving through the streets, motorcycles, vehicle horns. Poverty, especially along the river. Pollution. Crowded markets. A somber unhappy-appearing bride-to-be reluctantly selecting red silk for her wedding garment. The most influential downside, however, is the nearby site of Chu Chi Tunnels, though I am convinced if everyone in the world visited, and absorbed what happened there to both participants and nonparticipants, the chances of world peace might increase.

On the positive side, great street food, friendly people that want to please, a splendid lacquerware factory, interesting Chinese 'quarter', exquisite hot-stone massages and facials. No fancy spas, but these women know how to make a body feel terrific. Jessica indulges herself in a pedicure. But be damned if I am going to stick my foot into a lukewarm streetside bath. God knows what's in there. Good chance for a fungal infection. That is, if one survives. And with my luck those tiny carnivorous fishes would be extremely hungry that day and nibble more than loose, dead skin. I mean were the fish trained when to stop their feeding?

In spite of nonreligious inclinations, on a day tour, we visit a Cao Dai temple (a religion that incorporates Confuscianism, Taoism, Buddhism, and Catholicism). Equally as impressive as the stunning architectural designs are melodious chanting and obvious reverence and dedication of monks and disciples. The lifestyle appears humble and peaceful. I wonder if I could live here. I actually check into what is involved; one apparently studies several years through seven levels of ascendance to a higher consciousness and eternal bliss. However, since probabilities are that I won't live long enough to get through the first level, I quickly abandon that thought.

The last night in Ho Chi Minh Jessica and I indulge in a musical water puppet show, an ancient traditional art form. The performance is spectacular, the skill of the puppeteers amazing. Tonight, they tell a love story with various characters and scenes, all manipulated from behind curtains with underwater wires. Words are unnecessary. I have not forgotten the joy of love or impetuous hope. I join the little kids sitting on the edge of the platform at the front. Jessica remains in the second row; we are soon wiping tears of laughter from our aching cheeks.

Following the performance, if you can believe it, neither of us remembers the way back to the hotel and neither of us has the address. However, after a quiet dinner and our last shared bottle of wine, a patient taxi driver returns us to the general vicinity, and circles a couple of times until we spy the hotel.

We exchange reluctant, tearful goodbyes, knowing that our promises to keep in touch are unlikely to be fulfilled indefinitely, as each of us returns to friends, families, daily tasks, different lives. Our shared experiences, however, are uncommonly rare and must be treasured. I will never think of Vietnam without memories of Jessica, the only woman I ever met who is even more adventurous, more outlandish than I. A role model, if I ever had one. Now she could have inspired me to greater heights.

Pushing Boundaries: North Vietnam

After Jessica leaves for home in Australia, unhatched eggs still intact, I am on my own. I venture into the North, on an overnight train that threatens to shake out my teeth. Thankfully, they are still my own.

In the early light of dawn, a taxi van awaits to transport a few of us to Sapa. It is cold. Hell, I can see my own breath! Seems colder than Greenland! At least there I was prepared! Who expected this in an Asian country??? I cannot imagine why I thought coming here was a good idea. It must have been in one my 'less-aware moments'. However, from my room overlooking the valley, just before I catch a few hours of sleep, the rising sun casts a scarlet, golden glow on clouds that hover over floating mists below. All is not lost.

Sapa reminds me a little of Banff, Canada, or a resort town in the Swiss Alps without the luxury. Welcoming, yes. Comfortable, yes. However, it is apparent this is a growing tourist industry within a poverty-stricken area. Hotel and restaurant personnel do their best to please. In mornings and evenings, although both staff and guests must wear heavy sweaters or jackets in the open-air restaurant, there are always heaters placed nearby the diners. I cannot believe I am wearing a huge coat to dinner and enjoying it.

I soon feel I am part of the hotel 'family'. They teach me to cook Vietnamese dishes. Perhaps I should reword that to 'they try to teach me'. Of course, because food is involved, my enthusiasm and motivation for learning are apparent. And, when they "ooh" and "aahh" over my dishes, I pretend they appear and taste as good as theirs. Though, secretly, we all know better. It is a beginning.

The children of the family are delightful. We share hide-and-seek, hand games, and laughter, a common language to understanding. When, after a long day, fatigue sets in, I am served grand meals in my warm and cosy room, chicken baked in a coconut shell, or exquisite hot pot adorned with a carved feather-like egret. A goal to strive towards, with the knowledge I might never quite get there.

Which is okay. They know, and I know, I will not likely, once home, have access to coconut shells or egret feathers, but for a moment in time, we transcend limitations and seek possibilities.

At the bottom of the hotel steps, my first day in Sapa, I am immediately surrounded by a group of young women, teenagers or early twenties. Some have babies bundled on their backs. All carry wares, finely hand-woven embroidered textiles, beaded handbags, headscarves, baskets, linens, silver bracelets.

"You like? You buy?" one asks. Other repeat similar phrases.

"Velly beooootiful, you need? You buy from me?"

They soon speak over each other, and the cacophony grows, like a rock band warming up.

After bargaining, which they expect and, in fact, gleefully anticipate, I purchase a gorgeous blue and turquoise intricately patterned shoulder bag, and a smaller black evening purse, trimmed with red and golden braid and beads. Big mistake. The crowd of industrious young women immediately grows, moves in closer. Like someone caught a big fish on a hook and everyone wants to see, and go fishing in hopes of the same. I make an escape up the hotel steps and hide out in my room for several hours, trying to regain composure and figure out how to handle this. Their need is far greater than my ability to 'buy' and pack in my suitcase.

I decide to respond to future onslaughts, "No buy today. Maybe last day."

It doesn't work. About the third day I am in the market place searching for a certain dish I want to sample. So many women have gathered around me, I can't move. I turn to one of the women who is more fluent in English.

"Please, no more." She stares at me with questioning eyes.

"I want to buy things from you." I spread out my arm to include others. "I do not want to buy today. I will buy before I leave Sapa."

She asks me to repeat my request. She translates, and the women stare at each other in silence.

I continue. "I will not buy anything if you are 'pushy'.

"Pushy?" she asks. "What is pushy?"

I answer slowly, in short phrases, so that she will understand. "Yes, pushy is when you all come, say at one time, 'You like? Buy from me.' Pushy is when I say no, but you do not listen. You keep saying, 'Buy from me'. I have things to do. I cannot do them if you are all here. I cannot go anywhere. It makes me angry. I will not buy if I am angry. I will not buy if you are 'pushy'. If you are NOT 'pushy', I will buy before I leave Sapa."

She speaks in Vietnamese to her fellow cohorts. They stare at me, eyebrows raised, mutter to each other, nod, and gradually disperse.

For the next few days, they respect my wishes. I explore the town, enjoy scenic tours. In surrounding communities, I visit outdoor markets selling everything from live animals to pastries, textiles, household goods, tools, hardware, and Chinese plastics. Two young women escort me through their village, loan me a cloak and headscarf when the wind comes up, and arrange for a motorcycle ride back to town. They ask for nothing, though I tip them well.

The day before I leave, on my way to an ATM, I meet one of the young women. She thrusts her silver bracelets before me. They are poor quality. I shake my head. She tries with another. When I again refuse, she expectantly eyes me. "You say I not pushy, you buy. Three days, not pushy. Now, you buy?"

I bought. As difficult as it was to admit it, she had me. I bought substandard silver bracelets that I have since disposed of in a rummage sale. But I bought. She reminded me of something I learned a long time ago. Something my father taught me as a child. If you promise, you must deliver. That was my credo and salvation in all my years in education, especially working with children. Never make a promise you do not intend to keep.

In spite of these hassles, I grew to understand these women. They were attempting, in the only way they knew, to feed their children. Tourist numbers were down in February, and so were sales. I came to appreciate their hardships and respect their pushiness. I left Sapa with tearful good-byes, a suitcase full of embroidered textiles, and a heart full of love for them and their families. Where the men were I don't know, perhaps hunting, working the land, in day jobs, markets, or the Army. However, as was the case in tribal areas of northern Myanmar, it became clear that the women were the glue and touchstone of family and community.

I fall in love with North Vietnam, with its expansive, spectacular landscape, mountains, fog-filled valleys, snaking silver streams, winding, primitive roads and floating mists. With clear, brisk February air that stings one's cheeks and forces one's bare hands to seek refuge in woolen gloves or warm pockets. With terraced rice paddies and water buffalo, or oxen, pulling hand ploughs along steep slopes. And, if you can imagine, with a mama pig leading her tiny, black pot-bellied babies across the highway. But mostly with people, women in elaborate traditional, vibrant dress that varies with geographic area and tribal group, all warm, helpful, industrious, trying to scratch a living from this formidable land.

With a car and driver, recommended by my hotel 'family', I leave for a week-long expedition to the far north, travelling a huge circle from Sapa to the Chinese border, and back to Hanoi. We would pass through Ba Be, Ha Giang, Dong Van, Cao Bang, and Lang Son, among others, though these may not be in correct order of the route.

My driver, probably mid-thirties, with a wife and children, was a true gentleman, both respectful and protective, and spoke a little English. I lucked out. He even convinced guards on the Chinese border to let us cross a few feet into China (that may have been due to my encouragement), so I could say I walked on Chinese soil. More importantly, however, I wanted to view the vast, magnificent spectre of raw beauty of southeastern China.

The first day, as we enter a town, he asks, "Where you want to take lunch?"

"I don't know. You choose."

"What you like to eat? You like Vietnamese?"

"Yes," I reply, hesitating. "But no dog, no cat, no rat, no spiders, no worms." I accompany each of these with sounds, "ruff, ruff," and "meowww,", with hand motions, including s-like movements of a snake and fingers walking like a spider. To avoid misunderstanding, I shake my head vehemently.

He laughs, nods to communicate his comprehension.

"No snake wine?" he questions.

"NO, NO," I respond. "NO snake wine." Throughout Vietnam marketplaces, one can find dead cobras in bottles. They are supposed to be medicinal. On occasion, I have contemplated buying one to take back home, but I've never had the nerve. I envision the bottle breaking in my suitcase and the task of removing and disposing of a dead snake. Jessica's unhatched eggs suddenly take on a more positive light.

Subsequently, we frequent a wide array of streetside or indoor restaurants. He always goes in first, checks the kitchen and the menu, orders for us. Always, the food is delicious. When I add a pinch of the chili condiment, commonly placed on tables, to his heaping teaspoon, he questions, grinning, "A little more? No? You sure?"

I forget the names of the dishes within the first five minutes, but the overall impression remains. Sometimes I pay the bill, sometimes he does. Only once do we leave before eating; he takes my arm and leads me to the door, on the way out pointing to what seems to resemble snake, cut into rounds.

As we ascend into higher mountains, scenery becomes more spectacular, varies with each hairpin bend, eliciting gasps of astonishment and admiration. I lean forward in my seat, photograph through the windshield when I can. He pulls into roadside stops when he can so I can capture cliff faces, rock formations, winding rivers, and miniscule, toy-like villages. Around one bend fog rolls in, obliterates the landscape beyond and the valley below. I can barely see my own hand in front of my face.

"Photograph?" he inquires, with mischievous grin, eyeing the cloud cover.

I shake my head, "No. Same one. I have this one already."

We both laugh.

He provides information along our route, and stops at markets, allowing me time to wander and photograph, within guidelines for reaching our destination before nightfall. Sometimes he stays by my side, keeps a close eye on me, other times, he allows me to wander on my own. Because he is comfortable, so am I. I trust him implicitly.

In one market, I spend some time observing a middle-aged woman buying a female water buffalo from a man. Both of them seem to be accompanied by witnesses, who watch but do not take an active part in the transaction. As the buyer and seller speak in turn, the stacks of dong (paper money) on the earth in front of her gradually diminish as the piles in front of the seller grow. A female buffalo stands nearby, observing with huge 'cow' eyes, as though she has seen this before, and fears what is about to occur. A young one is pressed close to her side. I silently pray they will not be separated. Finally, the transaction is complete. The seller pockets his payment, hands the woman the rope tied around the buffalo's neck. The woman picks up her remaining money and thankfully leads away both mama and baby.

I wonder if she is purchasing the buffalo as 'dowry'. In this part of the country, when a young couple marries, it is customary for the family of the bride to pay the family of the groom, frequently in water buffalo, as compensation for removing an able-bodied worker from the family.

A few days later, we pass a roadside wedding. The driver stops the car, reverses, and parks on the shoulder. This one is modest version in comparison to two weddings I observed in the South. Those were all-day celebrations, held in huge wedding tents, complete with music, candles, flowers, feasting, and fashionably clothed guests. The bride married in a traditional Vietnamese red gown, adorned with gold-threaded lace, then changed to a traditional North American white gown for the reception.

In this case, if there has been a ceremony, we have missed it. My driver points out a woman in traditional elaborately beaded bridal garb, the groom by her side. A handful of guests, chatting and laughing, tidy the site, and strap wedding gifts, blankets, a few pots, pans, and dishes on to the back of a motorcycle. When I step out of the car, show them my lowered camera, the bride and groom grin, nod in agreement and very briefly pose for me. They exchange hugs and greetings with their guests, and hurry off, the bride and groom on one motorcycle, another young couple on a second. The driver explains that if the marriage is to have good fortune, it is the groom's responsibility to have his bride home before dark. A few other guests disperse on foot. A somber but resigned middle-aged woman, obviously mother of the groom, approaches a water buffalo, tethered nearby, unties and leads it down the highway. Both disappear into dusk.

The last few hours before we reach Hanoi are quiet. We both have our own silent thoughts as we prepare to go separate ways. In our week together, we have grown to be friends, with mutual respect bordering affection. He calls me 'little mama'. I am not sure why since, based upon the family photos he proudly displays, his own mother is smaller and more delicate than I. However, since this is the only time during my visit to Vietnam that I feel less than gigantic, I bask in the compliment.

He passes my luggage to the hotel doorman, embraces me, "Take care, little mama."

"You too," I choke, tears welling. He quickly turns, strides to his car. I know he doesn't want me to see his tears. Or perhaps he doesn't want to see mine. I am not only leaving behind a friend, I am leaving behind a country I have grown to love.

Sheila Carnegie

TEQUILA IN TEQUILA, MEXICO

"Experience is the best teacher, but the tuition is very costly."

Author Unknown

I had a bright idea, or so I thought at the time. Hell, as it turned out, it was one of the stupidest things I ever did and, believe me, there have been many. After summoning all the nerve I had within me, I rented a car in Guadalajara, or rather in Tlaquepaque, a town near Guadalajara, where I was staying at the time. I was going to drive into Blue Agave country the following day. I mean I could hardly visit the heart of mariachi music without visiting nearby distilleries in and around Tequila. The two go together like calypso and rum. Several of the buses had been stopped and robbed the previous week, and I thought a car rental might be a safer way to travel. Driving in Tlaquepaque appeared considerably easier than driving in Guadalajara. Besides, it wasn't as though I was planning on going alone. Two couples I met at the hotel, were game to go with me.

I am on my 'virgin journey' with Pepe (I nicknamed the Jetta 'Pepe' because it goes like hell). About halfway between the car rental office and my hotel, it happens. I hear the siren before I see the flashing lights in my rearview mirror. I mutter a few expletives. I pull over. The uniformed 'policia' saunters over to my car, leans an elbow on my open window frame, peers inside, eyes narrowed. He says something in Spanish.

"No, no hablo español," I stutter.

This time it doesn't work. He beckons to the police vehicle, and a second cop approaches.

"I speak to you in English," he offers. "You know you be speeding?"

"Well, yes, a little. It isn't really my fault. Pepe likes to go fast."

He raises his eyebrows, scans the car interior. "Where is this Pepe?"

I decide I'd better change strategies, before he hauls me off for being loony. "I wanted... I had to try out the car so I would know what it could do before I drove it in highway traffic..."

"Not a good reason," he chooses words carefully, "might I see your license?"

I rummage in my purse, reluctantly pass him the license.

He carefully examines the information, hesitates briefly before he asks, *"Colom-beeah?"*

I refrain from rolling my eyes. Here we go again. "Si. British Columbia, Canada," I answer.

"Breeteesh Colom-beeah? Donde?"

"Old Toad Island", I say.

He exchanges glances with his partner but says nothing, and continues writing out the ticket. I'm not sure if he hasn't heard of Old Toad or is only too familiar.

He passes the ticket to me, pockets my driver's license. The other policeman returns to the squad car.

Whoa!!!! There's no way he's getting to keep my license. My mind is racing. I must act quickly. I extend my hand toward his pocket. "My license please?"

"You pick up Monday when you pay ticket," he replies.

"But, but... I am leaving the country Sunday... see, here's my air ticket..."

184

He shakes his head, waves his hand like he is shooing away flies. I return the ticket to my purse. Well, to be honest, it was an airline ticket, but not one for Sunday. My courage has been boosted.

"You know I've spent big bucks in Mexico. Hotels, meals, clothing, shoes, sombrero, tequila to drink, tequila to take home, more shoes. I'm not exactly pleased right now. After all, I've been a good patron of your country. I've been here many times and have never been in trouble (well, as you know, that wasn't quite true, but I figured I could bluff him). And I will be back again; I absolutely love Mexico (I tried to sound convincing). At the very least, in the name of international relations, you could forgive me this small mistake and return my license."

"If you want your license, ma'am, you pay me 1200 pesos."

"1200??? No way. I know what the fine is for speeding. Besides, I wasn't going that fast!" I'm beginning to actually believe what I'm saying.

"800 pesos?"

I cross my arms, look him directly in the eye, "Try again. I'm not going anywhere." I'm on a roll.

"600 pesos?" he sounds hopeful.

"Nope. I will pay 400 pesos. No more."

"500?" he pleads.

I shake my head. "400 pesos," I am emphatic. "Nada mas."

We shake hands. I pull out 400 pesos and count them into his palm. He places my license in mine.

With a smile he warns, "No speeding." I nod, smile in return.

I cannot believe my good fortune. Maybe I reminded him of his mother, or grandmother. Maybe he was afraid of being reported for taking bribes. Or perhaps Sheila's spirit guides were looking out for me. At any rate,

I backtrack and immediately return the car to the rental agency. Enough is enough.

Oh yes, I still get to visit Tequila the next day. The five of us hire a tour van and spend the morning sampling more tequila than I can remember. Beginning at about ten in the morning. In fact, none of us seem to remember where we had lunch or what we ordered. Of course, the food may just have been non-memorable. And, to honour my commitment to the Mexican police, I buy a couple more bottles of the country's finest to take back to British Columbia.

There is a glitch however. Although I tore up my copy of the ticket, I don't know what the 'policia' did with his copy. It might still be floating around Mexico, with my name, address and license information, just waiting for me to cross the border. Better to play safe and avoid the country for the next while.

SNAPSHOTS FROM COTACACHI, ECUADOR

"Travelling – it leaves you speechless, then turns you into a storyteller."

Ibn Battuta

Sheila insisted. After her experience on the West Coast of Ecuador, our trip to Esmeraldas, she became convinced that all South American Latinos, especially men, are fine people, and she now resides in Cotacachi, north of Quito, in the Andes Mountains. She insisted I visit for a month or two, over the Christmas holidays, to experience joy and peace of the Yuletide season. Now those of you who know me, realize that although I am pretty much up for just about anything, I don't like Christmas. It reminds me of past tragedies. Personal ones at that. Probably that is why she persevered, so I wouldn't be alone, or so I could make some positive memories. Little does she know I'd prefer solitude and classical music during this season.

However, she is my friend. And considering the number of friends I have 'ticked off' in my lifetime, I am not anxious to add Sheila to that list. Although I must admit I came pretty close, on that trip to Esmeraldas, to removing her from all meaningful lists. Obliterating her forever, period. Anyway, we survived and here I am.

One of the first things I learned was that not all Latinos are fine 'guys'. In fact, so-called Colombian Immigration security officers (both male and female) stole cash out of my purse, in that place where you pass through the machine that exposes one's vulnerabilities as well as bones. Oh yes, they have a good thing going. While someone moved a wand of some sort up and down my body, producing beeps, no doubt caused from those ingrown earrings I swallowed an eon ago, someone else rifled through my stuff, out of eyesight, and lifted half my cash. They knew I was between flights and had to hurry, especially if I wanted to hit the duty free store. So much for potential affinity with Bogota.

The second thing I learned, after having landed safely in Quito, and being met by a very reliable driver, is that many Ecuadorian drivers are absolutely mad. We are driving on the Pan-American, which has more curves than the Monaco Grand Prix or the route to Tianmen Mountain in China, otherwise known as the Road to Heaven. I understand why. We weave in and out, as hairpin bends hug steep cliffs that drop steeply into deep ravines. Drivers pass on solid lines, at breakneck speeds. At times, three vehicles, sometimes including semi-trailers and buses, are coming straight at us on a two-lane strip of highway. Vehicles on both sides are forced to the shoulders. If I am lucky, I will reach Cotacachi alive, though it will not be without a migraine.

Drivers in Cotacachi aren't a whole lot better. The first morning, crossing a street, I almost get creamed by a taxi. Sheila yanks me back to the curb. "Drivers here do **not** honour pedestrians."

"No kidding," I reply, dry-mouthed.

"Yes, a guy in a wheelchair was killed last week."

Somehow, I am not surprised and silently wonder if the driver got extra 'points' for that. I swear drivers speed up when they see a 'gringo' trying to cross the street. Probably get extra points for us too. This does not seem like the 'kind and gentle' society that Sheila described.

"You can walk around at night," she encourages. "It's very quiet and relatively safe."

"Safe?" I query. "If it's safe, why do houses have bars on the windows? And why do property walls have broken glass all along the top?"

"Well, yes, there are robberies, but most crime is not violent."

"Driving like a madman isn't criminal? Killing someone in a wheelchair is not violent?"

However, I accept that she is correct about the town being quiet. In fact, after nine in the evening hardly anyone is on the streets (except for soccer games and fiestas, as I am later to determine. In that case, music often continues until daybreak). I relish the quiet. After a tiring journey, I sink into comfort, prop myself up with a feather-soft pillow. I definitely am looking forward to a good sleep.

Guess again. From 10 p.m. to midnight, more or less, neighbourhood dogs decide to settle their differences, or not. Seems a Golden Retriever from three doors down, out for his nightly run, has a bone to pick with the Mastiff-cross across the street. Both growl, yell, snarl ferociously and hit the metal gate between them with so much force I am sure the gate will be dented. Or if one of them breaks through... hell, you can be certain fur will fly and blood will be shed. This racket sets off two coonhounds who live on the roof next door, and attracts the interest of pretty much every dog in a six block radius. After a few hours, though it seems much longer, the raucous subsides. Either the owner retrieved his Retriever, or the master of the Mastiff hauled his dog inside, or perhaps threw tranquilizers out the window, before his neighbours did the same. At any rate, when the other dogs are no longer provoked, peace prevails once again.

At 1:13 a.m., just after I have finally fallen asleep, the first rooster crows. This sets off roosters all over town, several in fact in nearby yards, who continue to crow long after sunrise. Hell, the same thing happened in Mexico. I swear Latin American roosters haven't a clue when morning is to arrive, even though here, near the equator, it is pretty much the same time every day. You think they might have learned by now.

Just before six, the town awakens. Vehicles rush around, car horns and alarms sound, buses, roaring and coughing clouds of black diesel fumes, begin their routes. Nearby church bells, that sound like they might have 'gripé' (flu) begin ringing, and continue every fifteen minutes for some hours, especially if there is a 'misa' (mass) for someone who has recently died, or in commemoration of an anniversary of the death, the previous year or the year before that. Anyway, you get the message. Of course, as the town awakens, the dogs start up again, this time including a bunch of males fighting over a lone female that was thrust out on the street against her will.

About six thirty, the musical garbage truck begins door-to-door pickup, six days a week, I am told. Gas trucks, each playing different tunes, start their rounds that continue in alternating neighbourhoods throughout the day, trading full gas tanks for empty ones. I swear I will never again see a gas truck without musical notes strumming my brain.

From seven a.m., the school loudspeaker drones messages that no one, including Spanish speakers, can understand, and trucks advertising special events or selling brooms, or household goods, or corn, or potatoes, or toilet paper, begin shortly after that.

As I groan and pull the pillow over my head, I recall Juan Tonio's words to Sheila on our trip to Esmeraldas, and I realize two things. I am in another culture, and I am going to have to become a morning person, at least temporarily. Hell, to accomplish this could take longer than my entire vacation. I am amazed that

Sheila survives here. Maybe she uses earplugs. Maybe she has extras. Or maybe if I offer a financial incentive, or a few bottles of rum…

****

In spite of my first observations, Cotacachi gradually grows on me. It is in a valley between two quiescent volcanic mountains and for some unknown reason, positive energy is apparent. Perhaps it is the love story woven into folklore. Imbabura is deemed male, who has long wooed Cotacachi, female, and produced offspring, the surrounding mountains. When snow appears on the peaks of Cotacachi in early morn, the belief is that Imbabura visited her in the night. During my time here, Imbabura is a busy fellow. No one explains, however, the absence of new mountains, new children. Of course, given their age, infertility could certainly be a factor.

What appeals even more is the scenic agricultural area in which Cotacachi is situated. During the rainy season, surrounding pastoral hillsides have become green. Horses, cattle, and llamas graze the meadows. Cornfields stand tall, reach well beyond my height. Occasionally, cows are herded and horses are ridden down the streets. Each morning during the week, a father, resembling, I imagine, a Spanish conquistador without elaborate garb, and two children, all on horseback, pass by, while three or four dogs trail behind. The children dismount at the nearby school, the father, horse, and dogs depart in the direction from which they came. I know he will return shortly after noon, when the first staggered classes for the day are finished, and I watch for him. After the first or second bypass, he acknowledges my mesmerized attention by lifting his hat; I grin and nod in respect and delight.

The population in the area, including small communities around Cotacachi, is eighty percent indigenous, Quichua, descendants of the Incans. With the exception of the elderly, they speak both their own language and Spanish. Women wear traditional dress, long, dark woolen skirts, coloured embroidered white blouses with puffy sleeves, a hand-woven belt around their midriff, and a square woolen scarf, often folded in a triangle and knotted over the shoulder, in preparation for windy days or cooler temperatures. It doubles as a turban-like headpiece or headscarf against scorching midday sun. The traditional dress for men, white pants and shirts, scoured spotless on scrub boards, under navy wool poncho-type capes, seems reserved for parades and celebrations. Both females and males wear fabric, open-backed slippers strapped to their feet, which I suppose must be cold a good portion of time, particularly after sunset. Children sometimes wear traditional clothing; however recently they are more frequently clothed in school uniforms or modern casual clothing, jeans or sweat suits. I suspect this was a decision made by women, directly related to scrub boards.

Don't get me wrong. Their lives are neither glamorous nor easy. They work long hours on the land, in the rose industry or at labour jobs, are poorly paid, and score at the bottom of the long-established class hierarchy, lower than horses in fact. Many large families live in humble, over-crowded shacks, frequently thatched and bare-floored. On indigenous lands, they oversee their own justice systems, often based upon ostracism and restitution. Crimes resulting in death, however, including 'revenge killings', are the jurisdiction of national police and federal judiciary.

According to Quichua tradition, the good of the community is often placed above that of the individual. Their spirit of cooperation is impressive. For example, they frequently share or barter food, and have 'mingas' where men and women alike work together for road building, fire fighting, or other community improvement projects. We, in North America, could learn a lesson or two from them.

Cotacachi is renowned as the 'leather center' in Ecuador. The main street, 10 de Agosto, which honours the first movement for Independence in 1809, has been nicknamed 'Leather Street'. Throughout the country, different industries have been established in particular locations, based upon history of how craftsmen and traditional skills developed and emerged over years past. For example, traditional wood-carvers monopolize the nearby town of San Antonio, weavers in Peguche, textiles in Atuntaqui, traditional embroidery in Zuleta, and so forth.

We slowly meander down Cotacachi streets because, in spite of drinking coca tea, I have not yet adjusted to the altitude. Besides, one must maneuver one's way around dog poop where shopkeepers have not yet scrubbed the sidewalks, as they do each morning, or if it is five minutes after they have done so. At any rate, stepping carefully, it is easy to 'ooh' and 'ahhh' over a proliferation of shops, displaying shoes, boots, handbags, jackets, whips, saddles and other 'horsey items', basically all things leather. As is the case in North America, Asia, and likely most places in the world, clothing is tailored to petit, young people. Although there are many Ecuadorian women past the age of thirty or even younger, that outsize me, I know if I am to purchase a leather jacket, it will be custom-tailored, which they tell me they can complete in two days. I ask if the price is based on the amount of leather they will need.

****

We decide to have a late breakfast. Most expatriates in the area, and there are many, frequent a few restaurants that cater to North Americans. However, we pass an Ecuadorian restaurant that advertises *desayuno*, stop abruptly, and with a single mind turn back.

"I'd rather try an Ecuadorian breakfast," I suggest.

"Right on," Sheila readily agrees.

Once again I am surprised by how much she has changed since the Esmeraldas trip.

The menu includes some typical Ecuadorian breakfasts. Juice, coffee, bread with cheese and marmalade. Mote pillo, a garlicky hominy-egg scramble. Plantain dumplings. I note that encebollado, the popular fish soup that I love from the coast, is not on the menu. I remind myself we are in the Andes. Fresh fish and seafood are rare. We both order café leche; Sheila suggests humitas, a traditional dish that has survived from prehistoric times, steamed fresh corn cakes wrapped in corn husks; I ask for a boiled egg. In the Quito airport, I noticed a woman was served boiled egg, onion, and something else in a glass, and I hope this will be the same dish. I don't know its name, nor does Sheila.

I am surprised. The humitas are delicious, though a little dry. The boiled egg is wrapped in a washcloth to keep it warm, like one might a little chick. I think of Jessica and the unhatched eggs she was trying to migrate from Vietnam to Australia. *Pan tostada*, or toast is similar to a cheese biscuit, squashed flat by a sandwich press, egg-McMuffin style.

I am even more surprised when Sheila leaves the restaurant for a few minutes to get better cellular reception, and a Quichua male, extremely handsome in traditional dress, including a felt fedora-like hat, asks to join me. *Buen provecho (*equivalent of *Bon Appétit)!* Our conversation (translated from Spanish) roughly resembles an interview.

"I own a music company," he offers. "What work do you do?"

"A music company... what type of music?"

"Andean, but what do you work at?"

"I am retired."

"How old are you?"

"Old enough to be retired."

"Do you get a pension?"

"Yes, I do. How about you?"

He evades the question. "How much is your pension?"

"That is personal," I cut him off.

I am rather taken aback by his nerve, but have yet to learn that questions, considered bold by most North Americans, are common practice in Ecuador. I have also yet to learn that meeting North American women, all of whom are considered wealthy by Ecuadorians, is standard practice of various men, for various purposes, most financial in one way or another. However, in spite of the boost to my ego, for at least a few minutes, subsequent to my match-making experiences, my instinctive antennae twitches, and I offer no encouragement. Though I must admit both he and his hat would have been magnificent souvenirs of my trip. When Sheila returns to the table, raising her eyebrows, he makes a courteous and gracious exit. Her reputation as 'no fool' has obviously been established here, at least among the devious male population.

There are two open markets in Cotacachi, an extremely colourful one for fruits, vegetables, flowers, poultry, meats, seafood, grains and beans, spices and other foodstuffs. It includes a variety of eateries (Ecuadorian cuisine), and a huge dining area, as well as surrounding tiendas offering a variety of manufactured items.

The second, an artisan market, several blocks distant, sells various types of handmade clothing and crafts. It is a miniature version of the country's largest market, at Otavalo, twenty minutes by bus, which covers a block square on weekends, and several blocks on Saturdays.

Vendors in both haul their goods each day, to the market in the morning, unpack, then once again pack up all unsold items and haul them away in early evening. I don't know how they have the energy. I vow to support them, for their hard work, and surely I can find some souvenirs.

Vendors also frequent the streets, with baskets, carts, and even trucks, selling vegetables and fruits, fresh fruit juices, cheese, chicken or ground beef empanadas, grilled corn and skewered grilled meats, *cho-chos* (a type of bean with dressing) juices, *salchipapas* or *salchipapitas* (French fries with salsa and a miniature cocktail sausage), ice cream, and so forth. I bought the sweetest corn, which seems scarce in Ecuador, and juiciest strawberries, off the back of a truck. On the first or second day of my visit, as a 'green' tourist, I also purchased bananas from a street vendor.

"Bananas?" I ask.

"*Cuantos plátanos?*" she corrects me.

"*Dos* (two)," I reply, "*¿Cuanto cuesta?*"

"*Cincuenta centavos.*"

I nod, pull two quarters from my small zippered change purse, and hand them to her. She smiles, then reaches into her basket, presses into my hands, first one bunch of bananas, piles a second bunch on top. My arms are stacked high with bananas. At least a dozen and half bananas. What the hell am I going to do with all these bananas? How did I know that two meant two bunches and not just two bananas? I raise my eyebrows toward Sheila. She is laughing, but nods and whispers, "banana bread". I know that many bananas will make more banana bread than we will eat in a month. As we continue down the street, I hand out bananas to all the little old ladies with begging bowls, and offer them to kids, who quite enthusiastically comply.

By the time we arrive home, I have seven or eight bananas remaining. Great... banana bread, and the rest will provide opportunity for me to show off my flambé skills! Which I trust have improved since that party when I set my hair afire.

Eating patterns of Ecuadorians differ from those of North Americans. Breakfast (*desayuno*) is usually light. Their most substantial meal, *almuerzo* begins promptly around 1 p.m. If you try to order earlier, you pretty much wait until the allotted time before it is served, that is if the restaurant is open before 1 p.m. *Almuerzo* includes fresh juice of some sort, for example, *piña* (pineapple), *naranja* (orange), *cherimoya*, *guayaba* (guava), *guanabana*, *maracuyá, tomate de árbol* (tree tomato, which bears no resemblance to tomato), and *mora* (a berry resembling a combination of raspberry and blackberry). Except for those easily distinguishable, I doubt I will learn the difference among all of them any time soon. It is almost equivalent to learning a new language.

The lunch appetizer frequently consists of popcorn (*canguil*), as we know it, hard salted kernels unpopped, (*tostado*), or plantain chips, sliced thin and salted. Always there is a delicious soup. Each of the soups has a different name and individual ingredients. If one adds (or deletes) one or two different ingredients, it is no longer considered that soup. Similarly, particular names are given to main courses, which usually include meat or chicken, potatoes and rice, and maybe a vegetable or small salad. Sometimes dessert is included, other times not.

Between five and six in the afternoon, Ecuadorians snack on bread, cheese, coffee, and sometimes fruit. If there is *cena*, a larger meal similar to 'dinner', it is usually reserved for special celebrations held by wealthier Ecuadorians late in the evening. Or so Sheila tells me.

"Weddings, birthdays, anniversaries... that's when *cuy* is frequently served," she laughs.

"*Cuy*? What the hell is *cuy*?"

"Guinea pig..."

"Guinea pig?" I interrupt. I am not sure I accurately hear her. "You have to be kidding."

"Guinea pig. It is considered a delicacy here."

"Are there cages in the restaurant so you get to choose your own furry little critter? Similar to lobster tanks?"

"No, of course not."

"Well, how do I know? I never would have guessed guinea pig was a food, let alone a delicacy."

"It is one of the national dishes. Another is carne colorada... it is reddish pork or beef, marinated in achiote or annatto seed and beer. I know a restaurant where you could try both before you leave."

"Maybe the carne whatever... but I sure as hell am not eating anything that is looking back at me, or has its little paws folded in prayer, seeking salvation. I won't even eat fish unless it comes without head, tail, skin and scales and is shaped like a filet."

"Well, Sheila teases, "there are many other exotic dishes to try in Ecuador... beetles, grubs, cow innards, sheep brains..."

"Enough already," I interrupt.

That promptly ends our food discussion. I doubt that I will be hungry anytime soon, but, on the other hand, that would be a first.

****

About a week after my arrival, when I am beginning to be accustomed to the altitude, we decide to do some sightseeing. We travel by bus when we can. Sometimes we go to the terminal or wait at known stops, but if you stick out your hand, many buses will pick you up wherever. Usually we are the only 'gringos' on the bus.

We can't figure this out. Why would people want to pay $10 or $12 for a taxi when they can travel the same distance by bus for twenty-five or thirty cents? Of course, it might have something to do with various odours on buses, sometimes so crowded they resemble sardine cans upended, perspiration, musky earth, smells of sweat and toil, the occasional poopy diaper, and the scent of a nearby eucalyptus bluff.

However, buses are entertaining. Most of them have scalloped, fringed curtains, some with tassels. Several have mirrors, lights or vents framed with fur, dashboards covered with fake fur. All sorts of objects, tied above the windshield, swing back and forth as the bus moves, trinkets, baby shoes, crosses, rosary beads, a glass hummingbird, small furry stuffed animals, dream catchers, a topless hula dancer, photo of a burro. Items vary with individual buses and drivers; one even has a twelve-inch fuchsia crocheted hammock cradling a roll of toilet paper.

Come to think about it, that isn't such a bad idea. Chances are if you travel in Ecuador sooner or later, or maybe sooner rather than later, you will need to use a washroom void of toilet paper. Sheila says it is safer if you always carry it in your purse and, based on our experience in Esmeraldas, I know this to be true. I just never considered a shoulder strap, crocheted receptacle to house it. I just thought that was why so many of the leather handbags made in Cotacachi were large.

People, too, are interesting. Passengers, mothers, fathers, children, businessmen and women, shoppers, workmen, and students talk on cell phones and to each other. I'm not fluent in Spanish but understand enough to get the gist of their daily lives, unless their conversations are muted by music, which varies from romantic to modern, if one can call that music. Some indigenous, both men and women, double bent with weight, place huge loads of sticks, plants, produce, all knotted tightly in fabric, into the belly under the bus. Occasionally, there is a caged rooster, or a covered pail full of *cuy*. Since they aren't moving, I assume they are dead, but I resist peeking to see if they are prepared for feasting.

Vendors come on board selling ice cream, *chifles* (platano, dried and sliced like potato chips), chocolate, candy, other snacks, water, CD's, vitamins, and various gadgets and oddities. They ride a few stops until they finish their 'spiel', sometimes make a few sales, then scramble off the bus, cross the street, and mount the bus going the opposite direction. Occasionally, a passenger asks for money for a family member or friend who needs surgery or faces some other medical emergency. One day, the bus driver stops the bus, his assistant pulls out a huge machete, and by the roadside the two of them trim tree branches that threaten to scratch the paint.

Young people intrigue me the most, including those that have the courage to stand in the middle of the highway, performers, jugglers, or mimers, silently performing their stories for a few cents while cars whizz by on both sides. Hell, having witnessed Ecuadorian drivers, you wouldn't catch me out there for a prepaid trip around the world!

During subsequent weeks, we experience many sights and adventures. We visit nearby towns and artisan markets, both large and small, where each of several vendors claim to have the identical 'one-of-a-kind' item. From the boat on crater Lake Cuicocha, some 650 feet deep, hot bubbles can be seen rising to the surface and, frankly speaking, although the volcano has been dormant for some three thousand years, I can barely wait to get the hell out of there. Waterfalls at Peguche are spectacular, weaving demonstrations intriguing. A musical family performs on handmade Andean instruments. Lago San Pedro is quietly beautiful. With our heads in the cloud forest at Mindo, we revel in orchids and exotic birds; however, to be honest, it falls short in comparison with our time at the chocolate factory.

At Chimborazo and the Intag, we soak in cleansing hot springs, hoping to heal our bodies from foreign invaders, particularly those lodged from wine consumption or, in Sheila's case, rum. Mind you, based upon our trip to Esmeraldas, success might require several baths and several hot springs. A *Cofan* treatment from the Amazon rainforest includes an herbal bath soak complete with rose petals, facial massage, and a gentle body massage with bamboo switches, reminiscent of raindrops in the breeze. And after heavenly, warm and comforting mud wraps at *Termas de Papallacta*, I vow as a final request and last rite, to be swathed in Andean mud and thermal blankets. However, one must be careful of what one wishes... that could actually be the outcome of an earthquake, which are not uncommon in Ecuador.

There is no lack of entertainment here. It is just different from that in North America. Many parades and fiestas. Musical perfomances. Art exhibits. Seed exchanges. Cuisine demonstrations. Sports events. *Paseo de los Chagras*, a show of skill of both horse and rider, pride in a lifestyle that was borne on long ago haciendas and still exists. Bull fights, in the absence of picadors and toreadors, matadors face bulls with only capes, nothing more, except agility and ability to quickly escape. Restaurants that pop up overnight and as quickly disappear.

One of the highlights during my visit, though, has to be an evening of poker with the expat women's group. Such an event has its advantages, socialization, laughter, good food, but nothing beats (in my opinion) the photos of nude men on the back of the cards. Several of us frequently turn our cards to view various poses, no doubt a ploy of more serious players. I must admit, in spite of my enjoyment, I return home without winning even one hand.

Perhaps I will try to persuade Sheila to trade her cleaning 'woman' for a cleaning 'man', at least for the rest of my vacation.

****

No experience, however, is complete without spending the Christmas season in Ecuador. Prior to the holiday season, pilgrimage is not unusual. I am intrigued and somewhat inspired by such devotion to sacred ritual. However, when I discover people frequently travel huge distances on foot, let alone their knees, my interest suddenly, somewhat mysteriously, evaporates.

From somewhere around December 20th, or shortly thereafter, parades begin, preceded by fireworks that seem to indicate the parade route. Since we hear fireworks explode periodically for two or three days, sometimes a week prior to each parade, it seems, based upon my experience in high school labs where the male population delighted in making 'bombs', that they are being hand built and tested. This assumption is, subsequently, pretty much confirmed by smoke, sparks, and erratic explosions in various directions. I wonder, in fact, how many fingers have been lost in the process of setting them off. Or maybe it is like the bullfights, for those who can run fast, no problem. I respect the locals, who seem to have developed the skill of knowing exactly what distance to maintain during explosions. I do the same, plus add an additional several meters.

Nightly parades, accompanied by out-of-tune brass bands, begin before Christmas and continue until January 6th. Children, dressed as angels, form a large part in festivities, both in processions (Pase de Niño Viajero), honoring the travelling Infant Jesus, and in church services (novellas). Candlelight parades, accompanied by singing, A Cappella, are particularly poignant.

The Christmas Eve parade includes Archangel Gabriel, Mary, Joseph, newborn baby Jesus, wise men, angels and a live burro. The parade, however, is not without its problems. A few of the angels break into tears from exhaustion and need be carried. One child, a 'not-so-wise man' pees on the street corner. Well, better there than on his shoes, or on another 'wise man'. The burro inevitably exercises a stubborn demeanour and poops in the street. None of this, however, detracts from the significance of the occasion.

Nativity scenes dominate both parks, festively decorated with lights wound through tree branches. Although baby Jesus isn't usually placed until Christmas Eve, I never do see him the year I am there. We are told he did appear but mysteriously disappeared before morn. This does not bode well for Christianity or the spirit of Christmas.

The spirit of Christmas is epitomized, however, by the goodwill of a local merchant, who splurged on the very popular animal cookies and candies for local children. We packed a thousand bags over a two-day period. From the fire engine, 'Miss Cotacachi' and 'Papa Noel' tossed candies into the street. Kids lined up around the block to visit Santa and Mrs. Claus and collect candy bags. When the nine hundred mark was passed, and the line remained significant, the merchant made a quick visit to a local store that opened the door for the special occasion, and we rapidly put together another three to 400 bags.

Few Ecuadorians decorate their homes, except for nativity scenes and, if they give gifts at all, they are usually new shoes or pieces of clothing. Most kids, especially indigenous, neither expect nor receive toys. The expression on those serious little brown faces, their smiles and delight at receiving a few treats, such a small gift of hope, will always be with me. So little to one sometimes means so much to so many.

Of course, there were the usual criticisms by 'scrooges' who argued children shouldn't be given sugar. When the kids are drinking coke and eating ice cream for breakfast, does it really matter? And there were critics who considered the entire event detrimental to local cultural traditions. In my view, however, we are long past ancient traditions, which by the way included hunger and joylessness.

New Year's Eve did not disappoint. Shouldn't everyone drink champagne or *chicha* and frenetically dance in the streets this night? Less of the former and more of the latter? Shouldn't everyone watch a parade of masked men in drag, representing *las vuidas* (the widows) who beg for money, which I strongly suspect is 'beer money'? Shouldn't everyone clean their house from top to bottom, including blankets, curtains, floors, walls, ceilings, light fixtures, cupboards? Hell, maybe not that one. It pushes me beyond my limits. I suspect Sheila's too, but I dare not mention anything, just in case she gets a bright idea to follow the trend.

Shouldn't everyone burn effigies, scarecrow-like dolls, to signify all that plagued them in the previous year (*los años viejos*) and to begin a new year with a fresh mind and cleansed heart? No one escapes, neither politicians nor friends, bureaucrats nor lovers. One can even purchase effigies... in various sizes, shapes, gender, ages, hair colour and dress. They are laid out along the streets like dead puppets. A great idea, though I am afraid some years I might be burning until morning.

A few other traditions I don't get to witness... eating twelve grapes at midnight is supposed to bring good luck. Running around the block at midnight will bring enjoyment and success during travels. Wish I had known this before my Costa Rica trip with Dee. Wearing red underwear means you will find love... no wonder I haven't seen any in the store windows ... not that I have been looking, mind you. Yellow underwear is supposed to bring increased prosperity. So much for that. I mean, who the hell has ever bought yellow underwear? Or even seen it?

At midnight, hundreds of Cotacacheños, regardless of age, size, background, ascribed status, or political persuasion, temporarily abandon street dancing and swarm into the city square. A huge tower, constructed by volunteers earlier in the day, stretches into the starlit sky. At the stroke of midnight, the tower, also referred to as the 'castle' or 'castillo', is lit, flames snake up the sides and fireworks explode in all directions, lighting the heavens with spectacular brilliance. Streets vibrate with booming and cheering, relegating misdeeds, grudges and disappointments to the past, welcoming renewal and good fortune.

New Year's Day is very quiet. Music has subsided at dawn and by the time I am out at 9 a.m., more or less, streets have been already cleaned and are deserted. Even the dogs and roosters appear to have quieted. I remember wandering a sandy beach in Montego Bay in the silence of New Year's morn, and the astonishment and disbelief of the Jamaican beach cleaner who was concerned I might be lost from the night previous. Cotacachi reminds me that always on this day, I have reminisced the past year, symbolically if not literally burned my effigies, contemplated what I learned, anticipated what I have yet to learn, although always in spite of my reflections, the forthcoming year brings surprises I have neither envisaged nor predicted.

This morning, I consider my experience in Cotacachi. I've learned, contrary to Sheila's insistence otherwise, both mosquitoes and no-see-ums lead an active life here. I've learned that mañana does not mean tomorrow, but any time after today and possibly never. I haven't determined precisely when *Buenos días* ends and *buenas tardes* begins, though it seems to occur sometime between noon and 1 p.m., depending to whom one is speaking. Challenges are many and unpredictable. Some will try to take advantage if you let them. The word *tranquilo* is probably the most commonly spoken word in the country. The concept of family is sacred. Except when it comes to mistresses and in-family fighting, common worldwide. The word 'piscina' refers to a pool, not what some do in it. Never interrupt a soccer game, even in an emergency. There are more parades than there are official holidays. I've learned, perhaps most of all, if you dance in the streets with locals, reach out to individuals, enjoy their children and try to speak their language, they are helpful and in more ways than one, in ways you will never imagine, the experience will embed itself in your soul for all time.

Of greater significance, perhaps, I've learned it is possible to find joy and peace at Christmas without classical music and solitude. Sheila has been a wonderful hostess, and we have had a ball during our time together. Darn good thing, in fact, in spite of temptation, I didn't wipe her out in Esmeraldas. It seems somehow that she has mellowed my untamed, eccentric nature, and I'd like to think I have spurred her risk-taking. And she's dead right... most Latinos, including men, are fine people indeed. She has found her niche in Ecuador and is contented there. As for me, I am off to seek a new adventure. But darn, I hope she invites me back for Christmas next year.

ALSO BY SHEILA CARNEGIE

Dog Days and Nights, Humourous Adventures of Esmerelda Perkins, Book One. November, 2014. Best-selling ebook.

Readers, especially pet owner and lovers will delight in Dog Days and Nights, Humourous Adventures of Esmerelda Perkins, Book One, as told by fictional character Esmerelda Perkins, and written by best-selling author Sheila Carnegie. Esmerelda is inadvertently drawn into a friend's home to care for three cats, three birds, and to 'supervise' the breeding of a female Shiloh Shepherd dog in an 'amorous state of being.' The characters of the various critters are revealed, as are the dynamics of their interactions with both humans and each other. In spite of the problems Esmerelda encounters, you are sure to smile, and perhaps guffaw, at how she handles the situation. This story is based on an actual experience, although Esmerelda may have taken liberties in its telling, as she frequently does.

One reviewer wrote:

"I laughed until I nearly cried. Sheila's writing is so clear that I can almost see the action unfolding. There's a lot packed into this short book. I'm so looking forward to Book Two."

Tales From Old Toad Island, Adventures of Esmerelda Perkins, Book Two. February, 2015. Best-selling ebook.

This best-seller offers 260 pages of laughter as Esmerelda, in her unique and embellished style, speaks personally about commonplace events of life. She relates her impressions and experiences in moving to the island, and shares previously unspoken secrets and tales of resident characters and cultural adaptation. Stories about attempting to find her niche on 'Old Toad", as well as seeking a mate, for both herself and a friend are hilarious, as are her contemplations about aging and life in general.

One reviewer wrote:

"This book quickly draws you into a circle of friends who alternately shove and support the author, Sheila, into a new life on a small island off a bigger island off the West Coast. It winds its way through relationship, health, financial, travel and practical challenges with funny and poignant results. There were so many LOL parts dealing with the ups and downs of aging, and how to be mindful of friends and acquaintances but stay true to yourself. Doing so with humour and self-deprecation was the icing on the cake."

Beyond the Veil, A Personal Story of Spiritual Connection, June, 2014, Best-Selling ebook in three categories on Amazon.com.

Description:(**both poetry and prose**)

A spirit intrusion sets the author on a transformational journey from which there is no return. This is a true story of how Annabel Elizabeth Henley, who lived in the sixteenth century, reaches through time to relay a message of grave danger to her reincarnated lover. In so doing, Sheila is drawn into his circle of cultic mysticism. This journey leads to the realization of unbounded possibilities of the vast spiritual world and the conclusion that all of us are connected with spirit.

One reviewer wrote:

"Whether or not you believe in psychic experiences, this tale will take you on a riveting ride through time and space dimensions. The story is riddled with mystery, suspense and intrigue so skillfully written you will feel like a first-hand witness. The gripping intrigue, the breathless pacing of the story and characters are testaments to the power of words in the hands of an authoress clearly skilled in her craft."

--Sara Shank

Where Eagles Weep, Poetry and Verse from North America, West Coast and Central Canada. February, 2016. Best-Selling ebook for over a year.

Where Eagles Weep is a collection of free-form narrative, descriptive, and lyrical poetry and verse, set in North America, but relevant to the world. It is written over the past number of years, from the perspective and observations of a Canadian woman who grew up on the prairies and resided for some time on the West Coast. This is not "pretty" poetry. In several individual selections, the author addresses the "underbelly" of humanity, although she usually attempts to find the light that follows the dark. In one section, she masterfully tackles contemporary Canadian challenges, issues such as euthanasia, the Truth and Reconciliation inquiry into residential schools for First Nations peoples, the disappearance of women on the "Highway of Tears", the homeless and the lost. In other sections, she writes about regional life and culture, and about love, loss, grief, and immortality. As always, her writings emphasize the natural world and spiritual connotations, both thought-provoking and inspirational.

One reviewer wrote:

"Reading the poetry of *Where Eagles Weep* often stirred my emotions in ways few books of poetry have. No wonder Sheila Carnegie is the author of multiple best-sellers! She shares both light-hearted and deeply moving poetry inspired by topics making national headlines today as well as her life events. You must find some quiet, alone time to read and ponder this beautiful book of poetry and its relevance in your life today."

--Jan Myers, Best-Selling Author & CEO, LJM Publishing, LLC

Where Andean Condors Fly, Poetry and Verse from South America, Peru, Ecuador and the Galapagos Islands, January, 2016. Best-selling ebook.

Where Andean Condors Fly is a collection of free-form narrative, descriptive, and lyrical poetry and light verse, set in the Andes mountains of Peru and Ecuador, including Machu Picchu and the Galapagos Islands. It is written from the perspective and observations of a North American 'gringa' resident, over a nine-year period. Individual selections address a variety of themes, emphasizing the natural world, culture and traditions passed down through generations from the era of the Incans and conquistadores to their descendants, lifestyle, community events, love and loss, historical and geographical uniqueness. Common in her writings are humorous annotations and spiritual connotations, both thought-provoking and inspirational.

"*Where Andean Condors Fly* is a book of poetry that will leave indelible memories with readers. Sheila Carnegie has captured, with her beautiful poetry, magnificent places of Ecuador and South America. We are able to visualize, travel and enjoy these Andean landscapes and stories in an experiential and participatory manner. Its romantic, ironic, humorous and captivating style keeps us on the edge of reading and sensitizes us to perceive smells, colors, textures and Andean riches, invaluable and intriguing."

Katihuska Fransua Estrella Cortés, Ecuador
Degree in Languages, Communication and Literature

Dónde Vuelan Los Cóndores, Poesia y Versos de America del Sur, Perú y Las Islas Galapagos, enero, 2016, ebook más vendido.

Dónde Vuelan Los Cóndores es una colección de forma libre de poesía narrativa, descriptiva, lírica y de versos ligeros, ubicada en los Andes de Perú y Ecuador, incluidos Machu Picchu y las Islas Galápagos. Está escrita desde la perspectiva y las observaciones de una residente 'gringa' norteamericana, durante un período de nueve años. Son selecciones individuales que abordan una variedad de temas, con énfasis en el mundo natural, cultural y tradicional. Sucedidas a través de generaciones desde la época inca y de los conquistadores a sus descendientes, estilo de vida, eventos de la comunidad, amor y pérdida, historia y geografía con su propia singularidad. Lo común en sus escritos son las anotaciones de buen humor y connotaciones espirituales que provocan tanto reflexión como inspiración.

"*Donde vuelan los cóndores*, es un libro de poesía indeleble en las memorias de sus lectores. Sheila Carnegie ha logrado capturar con su hermosa poesía, lugares magníficos del Ecuador y Sudamérica. Nos hace visualizar, viajar y disfrutar de estos parajes andinos e historias de una manera vivencial y participativa. Con su propio estilo romántico, irónico, divertido y cautivador nos mantiene al filo de la lectura y nos hace sensibles a percibir olores, colores y texturas de una riqueza andina invaluable e intrigante."

Katihuska Fransua Estrella Cortés, Ecuador
Licenciada en Lenguaje, Comunicación y Literatura

Made in the USA
Columbia, SC
10 December 2017